Shakespeare's Avon

The History of a Navigation

by
Jamie Davies

THE OAKWOOD PRESS

© Oakwood Press & Jamie Davies 1996

British Library Cataloguing in Publication Data
A Record for this book is available from the British Library
ISBN 0 85361 490 3

Typeset by Oakwood Graphics.
Repro by Ford Graphics, Ringwood, Hants.
Printed by Alpha Print (Oxford) Ltd, Witney, Oxon.

**To Sue, whom I kissed on the banks of one river
navigation, proposed to beside another,
and married within sight of a third.**

In addition to its picturesque bridges, the Avon also sported a number of ferries, only one of which (Hampton, Evesham) remains in year-round service. This example is at Twyning Fleet, between Tewkesbury and Bredon, photographed early this century.
Almonry Museum Collection

Title page: Bidford water-gate in about 1900.   *Charles Showell*

Published by
The Oakwood Press
P.O. Box 122, Headington, Oxford OX3 8LU

Contents

A pleasure steamer (possibly *Jubilee*) at Cropthorne water-gate *c.* 1906.　　*J. Garrett*

Acknowledgements

Writing this book would have been very much more difficult without the generous help of the following individuals and institutions, to whom I am very grateful:

David Hutchings, UANT Project Manager, for spending a great deal of time answering questions, commenting on a draft of the manuscript, and providing many photographs; Dennis Hall, LANT Chairman, for providing valuable information about the Trust; WP Arman for papers about the UANT/LANT amalgamation debate; Elizabeth Barwell and Sonia Rolt for permitting me to use photographs from the collection of their late husbands, Hugh McKnight for providing photographic material; staff of the public libraries of Birmingham, Evesham, Gloucester, Pershore, Stratford-upon-Avon, Tewkesbury, Warwick and Worcester, the University libraries of Cambridge, Oxford, Manchester and Southampton, and the public and county record offices of Stratford-upon-Avon, Gloucester, Warwick and Worcester, for help in locating documents; the waterways museums at Gloucester and Ellesmere Port for access to archive material; the Newcommen Society and Birmingham Museum of Science and Industry for information about Jonathan Hulls' steam boat; Michael Brown (Birmingham Watercolour Society) for help in tracing copyrights; Reed Book Services for permission to quote 'Upon Eckington Bridge'; John Murray (Publishers) for permission to quote 'Inland Waterway'.

Most of all, I would like to thank my wife Sue for all of her support, and for patience beyond the call of duty when confronted with yet another wade to a muddy relic of a long-abandoned lock!

Jamie Davies
m.v. *The Saucy Mrs Flobster*

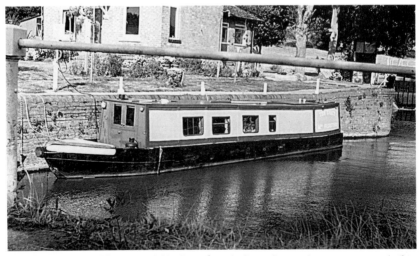

mv *The Saucy Mrs Flobster* moored in Strensham lock cut, Lower Avon.   *Author*

Chapter One

The Industrious Mr Sandys

It is a sunny summer Saturday in Stratford-upon-Avon. Shaded by the trees of riverside gardens, tired tourists take a break from their cultural tours and shopping expeditions to sit and watch the boats go by. In small skiffs and punts, hired by the hour, perspiring fathers row their families along the historic waterfront, their erratic courses punctuated by occasional collisions that provide high entertainment for spectating children. Through their midst glide elegant pleasure 'steamers', loaded with passengers enjoying a peaceful cruise from the busy heart of the town to the peace of the open country. Across the water, beside a sparkling weir, a few sightseers watch the chamber of a lock being filled. Inside are two narrow-boats, hired for the week from a company based on the Stratford Canal, which joins the river a little way upstream. Along the meadows facing the theatre, numerous yachts and motor cruisers have moored, many having come up from the River Severn, South Wales or the North Devon Coast.

This is the picture of the Avon remembered by the thousands who see it whilst visiting its most famous town - a wide, deep, busy, river, used by pleasure craft large and small, and giving enjoyment to all who sail its waters. The more inquisitive sightseer may, on understanding the significance of the lock and weir, wonder what the river would be like without them. Deducing that, in its native state, the Shakespeare's Avon would be much too shallow to bear large craft, he may wonder further at how it came to be made navigable in the first place, and why people took the trouble to make it so.

To answer these questions, one must look beyond the view from the meadows of a tourist town, to the Avon as it once was - an important trading artery which carried the cargoes of Midlands commerce even before the Industrial Revolution. This other Avon, this ghost from the past, has a great tale to tell. In its water's whispers are little-known biographies of transport pioneers, working a century before the canal age, and of their premature plans for social and economic engineering. There are stories of the changing fortunes of war and civil unrest, of visionary invention, and of bitter disappointment. In its shaded banks live memories of the generations of boats and boatmen who navigated the river through the ages, of the changing Avon Valley, and of the brave but hopeless fight for water transport in the age of rail and tarmacadam. In more recent times, its vale has been a theatre for the dramas of embryonic waterways restoration movements, to which the modern Stratford scene owes its very existence. First conceived before Shakespeare, the history of this navigation has its roots in another England, a feudal Kingdom still being shaped by the trades and the wars of the Middle Ages. To reach the sources from which it springs, we must travel back up the stream of the navigation's history to the 15th century, when one of the most powerful men in the country turned his thoughts to the advantages of a trading river.

In those troubled times, most of England's goods travelled on the back of a pack-horse, or in the hold of a small coastal sailing ship. With the old Roman roads in ruins and the seas poorly charted, both methods of transport were difficult and expensive, and as a consequence most communities were as self-sufficient as possible. Trade in the day-to-day necessities of life, such as agricultural produce and clothing, was centred on hundreds of market towns, each serving an area about 20 miles in radius. Travelling merchants would sometimes visit these, bringing with them 'foreign' goods which could be obtained only from other regions of England or Europe, and perhaps buying specialities of the region they had entered, such as high-quality wool, wine, or metals. With the country's pre-industrial economy starting, at last, to expand and recover from the plague years of the previous century, the benefits of improved transport were beginning to be realised.

With hindsight, it may seem strange that Britain, an island blessed with many large rivers, made so little use of them for the movement of goods and people. Indeed, for many centuries they had played their main rôle as a barrier to communication rather than an aid to it, and deep water was used as a means of dividing Shires and Kingdoms rather than uniting their merchants. Even where navigation was attempted, it faced many obstacles in the shape of shallow fords, low bridges, and weirs used for fishing and for driving water-wheels. As a consequence, most large rivers remained under-developed from the point of view of transport and only a few - the Severn, Ouse, Humber and Trent - were navigable more than a few miles from their estuaries. Even these were kept open only by explicit orders of the King. In 1352, Edward III had passed an Act (25 Edward III Stat. iv cap. 34) demanding the destruction of all fishing weirs on these rivers, and in 1430 the case of the Severn was strengthened by a second Act (Henry V cap. 2), declaring it the King's High Stream, freely navigable by all. This latter decree was of great benefit to the Severn valley, and the river rapidly became the major trade route from Bristol, then England's second city, through Gloucester and Worcester to the agricultural and mining areas of the Welsh Borderlands.

At about this time, Richard de Beauchamp (1382-1439), Earl of Warwick, first saw the potential of the river which ran past the walls of his great castle. Wishing to develop further his power-base through economic, as well as military might, he planned to increase the importance of his town to the merchants and traders of the English Midlands. To this end, he decided to make the Avon navigable, '. . . that smale vessels as the water would bere myght be conveyed from Tewkisbury to Warrwick'.

Were his ambitions to be fulfilled, his people would have witnessed

> . . . a plesant syght of the vessels coming and a makying to Warewick and all the Countrey, and a grate profit to the Lord is in carriage of there wynys and odre stuff from Bristow by watre and causid merchandis the better willyd to dwell in the town.

It was a courageous and optimistic plan, but there is no historical record of anything of the sort coming to pass - there is not even evidence of work beginning. That this should be so is hardly surprising- such a project was quite unprecedented, and it was not until well into Elizabeth I's reign that the first large-scale river improvements were undertaken (pound locks on the Trent and Lea). Possibly, de Beauchamp had underestimated the work required, though even if he had understood how much had to be done, other circumstances were against him. Henry VI's reign was a turbulent time, with the English driven from much of their territory in what is now France, and domestic feuds, which were to become the Wars of the Roses, undermining the country's stability. Richard de Beauchamp died in 1439, and his successor (Henry de Beauchamp) may not have shared Richard's enthusiasm for the scheme. In any case, 10 years after Richard's death, Warwick fell into the hands of the Nevilles, the 'Kingmakers', who gained political power by more direct routes than stimulation of local trade! For one reason or another, the scheme was dropped.

Later, as the national economy slowly expanded through the Tudor and early Stuart ages, there may well have been others who saw in the Avon a means of moving their goods for great profit but left no record of the fact. The first real sign of action came in the 1630s, when Letters Patent were at last obtained for making the river navigable. The arrangement was unusual for the time, placing the burden of the work not on a number of commissioners, but rather on a single young entrepreneur, William Sandys. Born at Ombersley in 1607, the second son of William Sandys of Miserdon (Gloucestershire) and Margaret Colepepper, Sandys lived in the village of Fladbury, situated between Evesham and Pershore and on the banks of the Avon. The Sandys (nowadays pronounced 'Sands') were a powerful family at the time, and their name is still commemorated in street and pub names in Worcestershire. In the 17th century his father's wealth enabled William to complete his education at Oxford. His choice of college, Gloucester Hall (now Worcester College), may well have been crucial to the development of the Avon; one of the few people in the country with experience of building and maintaining a navigable waterway happened to be the College Principal.

At the beginning of the 17th century, England's longest river, the Thames, though having the potential to be an excellent transport artery westwards from London, was in practice almost unnavigable in the upper reaches. With no locks to maintain water levels, and several shoals in the river, even the fairly small vessels common at that time could reach Oxford only at times of very high water. In 1607 a Commission was set up to improve the situation, but little was achieved and in 1623 a new Commission was formed. This group, which included John Hawley, principal of Gloucester Hall, managed to make great improvements by building locks to raise the water over shallows at Clifton Hampden, Sutton and Abingdon. The locks at Iffley and Sandford were the first to be built, and were completed by 1632. Having gone up to Oxford in 1623, Sandys might have been able to observe in detail the planning and execution of the Thames works. What he learned there could be applied to the river flowing through his native Fladbury with even greater effect, since it had never been navigable even in the wettest months.

The rewards for the proprietor of a navigable Avon would have looked most promising. The roads, which formed the only means of transport, were then very poor and badly looked after. Their maintenance was performed by parishes through which they passed; according to an Act first passed in 1554

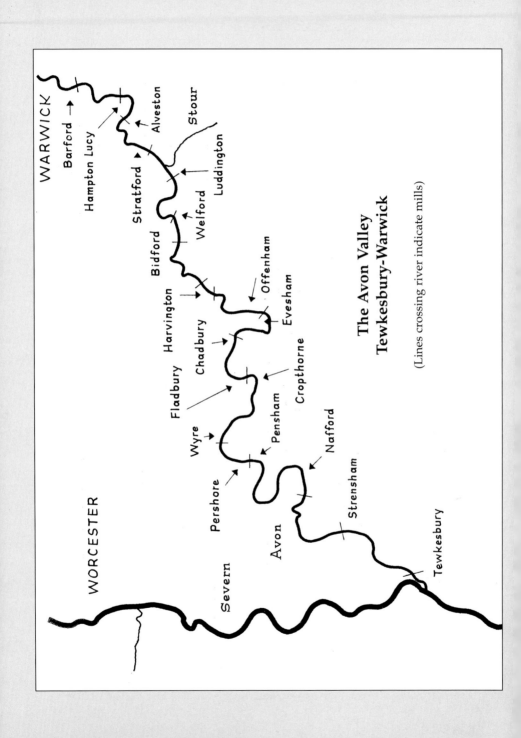

The Avon Valley
Tewkesbury-Warwick

(Lines crossing river indicate mills)

(2&3 Philip & Mary cap. 8), every able-bodied parishoner had to spend four days per year on roadworks. In 1563 this was increased to six days in an attempt to halt the decline in the standards of repair. The system worked very badly; involuntary labour was done only grudgingly, and the surveyors were employed for only a year so failed to build up any expertise. David Bourne described the resulting tracks as 'more like a retreat of wild beasts and reptiles than the footsteps of Man'. Many parishes were fined for their shoddy work, and just before the outbreak of the Civil War no less than 24 such indictments were served in the Vale of Evesham alone. Thus the cost of transport was very high compared to that which could be achieved by bulk cargoes on the water. An example which illustrates this point clearly comes from the salt trade from the North of the county - in 1699 the cost of transporting one ton of salt by road from Droitwich to Worcester, a distance of about 9 miles, was the same as that of then transporting it by water about ten times as far from Worcester to Bristol.

The economic geography of the Avon valley promised a wealth of potential trade. The lower part of the river passed through the rich farmland of the Vale of Evesham, which would be able to export crops as well as import fuel and building materials. Higher up, the city of Warwick would be able to communicate with the sea, encouraging traffic in high-value merchant goods. Higher still was the Coventry coalfield, a relatively new mining area in desperate need of a means of exporting its product cheaply. Before the 1550s the profits of the whole field were less than £5, but after a 1591 survey had revealed a new coal seam, mining activity increased and by the 1630s Bedworth colliery produced more than 20,000 tons. A navigable waterway allowing transport of this coal to the rest of the country, and also to sea-ports, would have been immensely valuable. Indeed, in a later submission to Parliament, it is said that merchants of Coventry first approached Sandys with the idea of a navigable Avon.

It is interesting to note how the anticipated pattern of trade had changed since the plans of Richard de Beauchamp; downstream mineral traffic, rather than upstream luxury goods, was now a major justification of the river's improvements. In addition to the obvious source of revenue - river tolls - there was the potential for massive profit to be made through the economic development of a region supplied with better transport. Centuries later, this general stimulation of local trading justified the building of many branch railways; they were never meant to pay their way alone, but rather to increase their promoters' wealth by aiding other businesses in which those men had a stake. In modern times, this is conveniently forgotten by those who close lines because they don't pay their way, though it is of course remembered when a motorway, which never pays its own way directly, is being built to places once served by water and rail.

When, in the early 1630s, Sandys started to make the Avon navigable, he immediately ran against the opposition of others who had an interest in the river and its meadows. First, land had to be purchased, for use as a towing path and also for the locks and sluices required for regulation of water level. Many riparian owners asked very high prices for their land, and some would not cooperate at all. If landowners were obstructive, millers were worse. Water mills, of which the Avon sported a large number for a variety of industries (*see map page 8*), rely for their power on carefully maintained differences of level across a weir. Their owners were therefore extremely resistant to any change in these levels as boats passed the weirs, and the common flashlock (*see page 12*), which relied on draining the pound above a weir for its action, would have reduced their profits greatly. Most owners of such water-mills were therefore deeply suspicious of a navigation.

The difficulty of his undertaking soon proved too much for the limited personal resources of Sandys, and the opposition of riparian landowners prevented further progress. His solution was to appeal to Government for Letters Patent for his Navigation, which would effectively give him the legal right to compulsory purchase of land. His request was answered on 9th March, 1635:

> Whereas Mr secretaries Windebanke did this day acquaint his Majesty that Wm Sandys of Fladbury in the County of Worcestershire, Esq, had undertaken at his own costs to make the River of Avon passable for boates of reasonable burthen from Severne where that river falls near Teuxbury . . . unto or near the Citty of Coventry, and that he hath already been at great charge in his endeavour to bringe the work to perfection . . . and the board affirms verie well the good affection and endeavours of the said Mr Sandys in undertaking so commendable a works as well for the good of the public as himself and willing to give him all possible encouragement did this day . . . order . . . special Commissions should be issued under the great Seale.

The Royal Commission consisted of the following 30 members;

Viscount Campden	Lord Windsor
Lord Spencer	Lord Brooke
Lord Craven	Thomas Coventry Esq
Sir Robert Barkeley	Sir John Bridgeman
Sir Richard Tracey	Sir Thomas Purkeiry
Sir Walter Devereux	Sir William Russell
Sir Edward Littleton	Sir Thomas Lucie
Sir James Pitt	Sir John Roy
Sir Robert Lee	Sir Robert Peyto
Sir Edward Underhill	Sir Robert Tracey
Sir Robert Cooke	William Smith D.D.
Serjeant Ward Esq	William Sheldon Esq
Richard Cressheld Esq	Walter Overby Esq
Humphry Sally Esq	William Bailey Esq
John Keyte Esq	

To enable them to fulfil their duties of encouraging and supervising the improvement of the Avon, the commissioners were enpowered to examine witnesses under oath and to survey the river and its works. They were to listen to objections of any opposing persons, and to make judgement in cases of dispute; if their rulings were not accepted it was their duty to warn the plaintiff that he would incur the displeasure of the Court, and if he still objected he was to be referred to the Privy Council where 'such further order shall be taken as shall be fit'. Most of the commissioners were either neutral to the scheme or stood to gain from its stimulation of the Valley's trade. However, one of its members was openly and vehemently opposed to Sandy's ambitions - he was Sir William Russell, whose large estate included the mill at Strensham.

By the time of their first public meetings, the commissioners seem to have divided the river, for administrative convenience, into two sections with Stratford as their common boundary. To facilitate the works on the downstream section, a Royal summons called Winsdor, Peyto, Cooke, Bridgman, Devereux, Pitt and Berkely to a meeting at Evesham Town Hall on 30th August, 1636. Their report recommended a scheme involving 13 'cuts' (locks and their associated channels) between Tewkesbury and Stratford-upon-Avon (*see map page 16*), the section of the river north of there being outside their brief. A rate of 40 shillings (£2) per acre was fixed for land which was to be purchased for either cuts, or for the 'landway' (towpath). No lock was to take more than one acre, the setting of such a limit implying that true pound locks were to be built (see below). The width of the landway was to be restricted to 1 ft 6 in., and rates of compensation for millowners were also fixed.

Sir William Russell refused to associate with the Commission's reports, 'having, as he said, more concern as party', and devoted himself to obstructing, rather than facilitating, Sandys' work. His reasons are not recorded, and may have varied from a personal vendetta, to concern that his own mills would be disrupted, to a possible rival scheme of his own. The efforts of the other commissioners did little to diminish his implacable opposition, which eventually found physical expression in the 'battle of Strensham Mill'. Perhaps predictably, there are two conflicting accounts of the important events. According to Sandys, a boatload of his men had been sent there on a surveying expedition. On discovering them on his stretch of river, Russell became angry and he 'did cause them to be twice assaulted and the boate to be taken away, some of the petitioners escaping not without danger of their lives'.

Giving evidence to the Attorney General, whose help had been enlisted when Sandys appealed for justice to the House of Lords, Russell denied the story, alleging instead that three 'strong persons' went in a boat to Strensham Mill and violently assaulted the old miller there.

Their Lordships declined to choose between the rival accounts, preferring to reach a compromise to prevent future strife, recording that:

Sir William Russell on Friday Last did declare at this board he doth seek not to oppose but only desires that satisfaction may be first given him for his particular interest which Mr Sandys professes himself very ready to do according to the value thereof . . . Their Lordships being desirous that soe publique a work may recive noe interruption or opposition . . . doe pray the Lord Privy Seale to call the said partyes before him and both to take order for the restitution of the boate and to resolve all the other differences without troubling the commissioners if it may be, and to make work an amicable agreement between the parties as that so a laudable a work and undertaking may receive no stop or prejudice by private dissention.

Whatever arrangements had been made between the Lord Privy Seale and the two antagonists, they produced little more than a cosmetic peace, and the men continued to annoy one another. In September, Russell complained that he

A typical early flash-lock, in this case from the Upper Thames.   *T. Robertson*

Impression of a typical Avon Barge in the time of William Sandys. The drawing is based on a combination of sketches and wood-cuts in Stratford and Evesham libraries, and vessels operating on other navigations in the 17th century.   *Author*

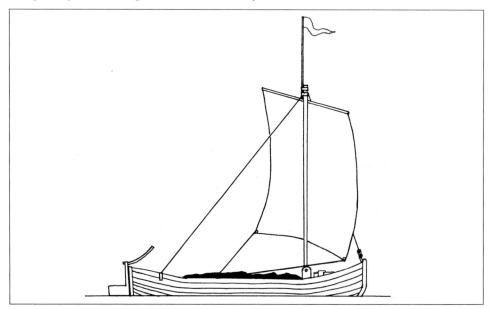

could no longer get any of his warrants executed in the Hundreds of Oswaldstow and Pershore, in which William Sandys was baliff. In retribution, he imprisoned two of Sandys' deputy baliffs, who in November petitioned the Lords to help them. By this time, the report of the Evesham meeting had been made, and it contained references to Russell's opposition to the river scheme. He had complained to them that Sandys' men had again been aggressive, this time saying that they had cut his turf without permission, and that he would oppose the scheme not just for his sake but because it would harm the country as a whole. This last point was perhaps the most contentious and controversial of all of the Knight's claims, implying that the decision of the King to grant Letters Patent was faulty. The commission's report to Charles I underlined Russell's apparent disloyalty by reminding him that the net benefit to the country was 'already determined by your Majesty's great judgement'.

The day after they had left Evesham, the commissioners went to meet Sir William Russell at Strensham Mill, where one of the planned locks was to be built, to deal with another bone of contention. The lock would have cut off the route from the mill to nearby Eckington (often impassable anyway), and Russell objected to this even though Sandys had offered to build a bridge. Sir William never arrived, and a servant of his was sent to say that he would be late. After waiting two hours, the members of the commission went to Tewkesbury to see Russell's agent, the attorney Richard Dowdeswell. He said that Sir William was now objecting on the grounds that the improvement of the Avon would cause the Severn to flood, a view dismissed as nonsense.

The only other objections noted on the report were from Edward Pratt of Pershore (who supported Sir William) and Thomas Copley and Thomas Saunders, both yeomen who wished to prevent the landway from crossing their fields. This was by no means irrational prejudice, as the gangs of bow-hauliers who would pull the boats were known to be rough on other waterways, and apt to steal 'Hennes, Geese, Ducks, Piggs, Swannes, Eggs, Woode and all other such commodytes'. In fairness, not all were scoundrels; another writer had said 'I know many water-men, and I know them to be like other men, some very honest men and some knaves', but obviously yeomen were best advised to keep their land to themselves. Of the three objectors, Pratt was the most energetic and he organised a petition in support of Sir William. The matter was resolved on 27th November, 1636, when a council order committed Pratt to Fleet Prison during His Majesty's pleasure, and summoned Copley and Saunders to answer for their action. Sir William and his attorney were warned that they would have to face the council in one year's time unless they gave up their opposition and went along with the other members of the commission. This last harsh edict seems to have spelt final victory for the navigation, and its detractors fell silent.

Winning this conflict must have been a difficult feat for young Sandys, and in his 1911 article on the early history of the Avon, the historian Feek suggests that bribery was almost certainly involved. At that time, King Charles I was very short of money, and some sort of 'donation' would have been very welcome. No records of this transaction seem to exist with respect to the King, but a memorandum implies that some obligation towards Sandys was felt by Mr Edward Nicholas, one of the King's secretaries, who tried to prevent Sir Edward

Alford, a riparian owner, from getting more money for his land. The bribery, if it happened, rebounded on Sandys years later when he was banned from standing for the Long Parliament.

In spite of these problems, work had apparently progressed well, away from disputed areas, and the report mentions that the commissioners had seen 'one of the sluices made by Mr Sandys'. The going was troublesome and expensive, but the way to Stratford was apparently opened by 1639. A contemporary account is given by the Worcestershire historian Habingdon (*see map page 16 for lock sites*):

> The Industrious Mr Sandys, beginning his unexpected design in March 1635, did in three years make it [the Avon] passable for barges of 30 tons from the Mouth . . . to Stratford upon Avon, being about xx miles by land and xl by water, through foul and low bottoms, and especially though the deep Vale of Evesham, purchaseing with excessive charge mills, meadows, and other grounds to cut in some places a course for this watry work . . . he made sluices at Tewksbury Co Gloucester, Strensham, Nafford, Pearshore, Piddell, Flatbury, Chadbury, Evesham, Harvington, Clive Prior, Bidford amd Welford; and soe wrought by his sluices keeping upp the water in the summer as these barcks may then come above Pearshore, when they cannot for want of water reach Worcester.

This last sentence is indicative of the very poor state of the Severn at that time, which was still in its natural state. Being the 'King's High Stream of England', it was toll-free and therefore nobody stood to gain by improving the river and recouping the outlay from tolls. The upper reaches were dependent on the tide and rain for adequate water (which they would get for about 10 months of the year, before 20th century flood control ruined navigation above Bewdley). The lower reaches were beset with 'rockes and perilous deepes, whirling gulfes and violent streames'. The lower reaches of the Severn affected the Avon too, because they formed its only link with the sea. However, the latter river could compete with the summer Severn for much of the trade north of Tewkesbury because of low water in the larger, but unimproved, river. Habingdon continued:

> . . . neither meaneth Mr Sandys to set at Stratford upon Avon the bound of his labour, but intendeth (if it may be) to extend the same up to Warwick. And for the expense which he hath hereupon bestowed, it cannot be valued soe littel as xx thousand pounds.*

Because of the limited brief of the commission, there seem to be no official records of work which may have taken place upstream of Stratford-upon-Avon. Steps in the riverbank at Charlecote House and Hampton Lucy Church indicate that short-distance passenger travel may have been common even before Sandys, and a circular pool at Hampton Lucy Mill Weir is probably the site of an old lock chamber; these constitute the only surviving physical evidence of navigation towards Warwick. Although the travel enthusiast John Taylor wrote in 1640 that he could reach within four miles of Warwick, this was in a small boat and not a cargo carrying vessel, so gives little indication of the state of the river. Because of references in later histories, some writers have doubted

* This estimate is probably a great exaggeration.

whether Sandys even managed to get as far as Stratford, but Habingdon is very clear on this, and other sources would appear to agree. For example:

> . . . the said Mr Sandys imployed much time and expence to advance the work to Stratford-on-Avon, which is above halfe the way to our said Citty of Coventry; and had then proceeded to finish to the same had not the supervening troubles of the nation interrupted him.

The confusion seems to have arisen from accounts of the reopening of the navigation in later years. Habingdon's comment that vessels could reach Pershore (rather than Stratford) in dry summer months suggests that much work remained to be done before year-round navigation would be possible throughout. In later years, more locks were built, especially at the upper end of the river.

Unfortunately, there is no accurate account of the engineering works, and only Habingdon records the of siting of weirs (*see map page 16*). From other sources, such as artists' sketches and drawings, the following can be supposed, with some reasonable confidence.

The largest cargo boats weighed about 30 tons (just less than a loaded narrow-boat) and were wide, flat-bottomed barges which carried a single square sail. On the Severn, there were two principal vessels at the time, large 'Trows' of 40 to 60 tons, which were about 50 ft by 18 ft (about the size of 'Pinta', which travelled to the New World with Columbus), and smaller barges of about 30-40 ft and 10-30 tons. The Avon craft were probably examples of the latter type, and may well have been built at boatyards at Tewkesbury which had experience in building for the Severn. When not using the prevailing south-westerly (upstream) wind power, which is in better supply on the lower reaches, the higher parts of the river being more sheltered, the boats were man-handled by teams of 'bow-hauliers' from the landway. Horses were never used. Old woodcuts record the shapes of these vessels, and they are also remembered, with a little artistic licence, in the sign of the 'Navigation Inn' at Evesham. Because the size of vessel able to use a navigation is usually limited by the sizes of the locks, it is fairly safe to assume from boats illustrated in the woodcuts that the original locks were therefore of about two-thirds of the capacity of the present ones.

The building of locks and weirs, would, of course, have been one of the major challenges faced by the builders of the navigation. In the simplest case dams, the construction of which was already well-understood by mill-wrights, were placed downstream of shallows to hold back and therefore deepen the water. While most of the structure was permanent, a portion could be removed to allow boats to pass. In early examples, this section consisted of paddle-shaped planks attached to a frame, and it was dismantled completely when a boat passed through. Crews bound upstream would haul their vessel past the weir, replace the planks of its temporary section, and wait for the water to build up enough depth for their needs before continuing. Barges heading downstream could pass through the opening in the weir as the previously-impounded water was draining away, and ride the resulting 'flash' for a considerable distance

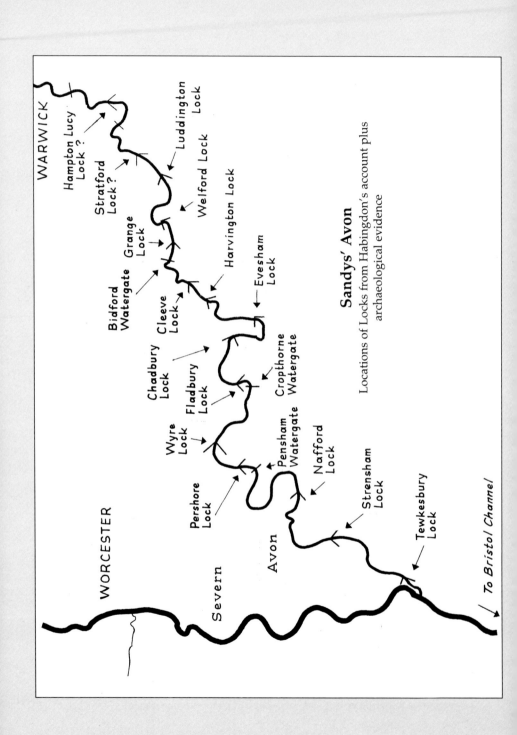

Sandys' Avon

Locations of Locks from Habingdon's account plus
archaeological evidence

WARWICK

Hampton Lucy
Lock ?

Stratford
Lock ?

Luddington
Lock

Grange
Lock

Welford Lock

Bidford
Watergate

Harvington Lock

Cleeve
Lock

Chadbury
Lock

Evesham
Lock

Cropthorne
Watergate

Fladbury
Lock

Wyre
Lock

Pensham
Watergate

Nafford
Lock

Pershore
Lock

WORCESTER

Strensham
Lock

Severn

Avon

Tewkesbury
Lock

To Bristol Channel

downstream. Such a precarious practice gave these primitive 'flash-locks' their name. Flashes from a weir upstream of a grounded craft could also be used to create a temporary increase in depth, freeing the boat at the expense of an enormous waste of water. In later examples, the weir was equipped with sluices to control the water, and a movable gate across the navigable passage - these were generally called 'water-gates' or 'wyres'. The gate was arranged so that it was held firmly closed by water pressure, and could be opened only when the head of water had been entirely released. Sandys may have used either design, or both. The water-gate at Bidford is illustrated on the title page.

Where a weir had already been constructed to power a water-mill, flash-locks were less practical because of their interference with the miller's precious water levels. A more sophisticated approach was the pound lock, introduced to England in 1563 (Exeter), and still in wide use. In its traditional form, it consists of a chamber, the opposite ends of which communicate via gates with the river above and below the weir. These have one or more holes, which can be closed off by wooden paddles placed on their upstream sides, water pressure ensuring an acceptable seal. Crews bound upstream manouevre their craft into the chamber. The lower gates are then closed, and the upstream paddles lifted to admit water to the lock. Once its level has reached that of the river above, the top gates can be opened and the vessel may proceed. Downstream crews simply reverse the operation. Wasting only one lock-full of his water, rather than draining miles of river, the pound lock would have been far more acceptable to a miller and was the type installed wherever navigation and water-power conflicted. The Avon's early pound locks had circular, rather than rectangular chambers to distance their walls from the turbulence of inrushing water. This shape is still reflected by the diamond chamber at Wyre Piddle (*see pages 91 and 100*), and the ruins of Cleeve lock (*see page 144*).

The effects of Sandys' river on the area and its development are unclear from any objective sources, due to the disruption caused by the Civil War which so closely followed its opening. However, Habingdon again provides us with his own observations;

The benefitts which arise to this country by this watry work . . . are such as all may see them, and the neighbouring inhabitants receive them, among the number of which I will recount this only, that whereas the Vale of Evesham laboured heretofore with extream want of fewell, and thereupon was inforced in these exceeding foul ways [the roads] to fetch coales from far remote places, Mr Sandys hath with his labour so contrived as very many of them hath coales delivered them at their doors, and others somewhat further off have easy access to them.

As well as direct economic benefits, the works provided some degree of control of water levels and helped to prevent the severe flooding which did a great deal of damage to villages on the banks. According to some sources, Sandys' home village, Fladbury, took its name from a corruption of the word 'flood', being originally called 'Fleodanbyrig'.

By 1649, Sandys applied for Letters Patent to allow him to charge an additional toll of 1s. per ton on coal, in an effort to recoup some of his outlay. In October of the same year, there is an entry in the minute book of the Stratford

Water-gate

These were built near shallows (e.g. the old fords at Bidford and Pensham) where no mills relied on a difference in water level being maintained.

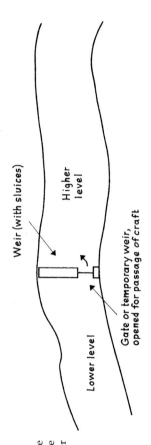

Weir (with sluices)

Higher level

Lower level

Gate or temporary weir, opened for passage of craft

Pound Lock

These were normally built at mills, to conserve water level differences for the miller. Early references to Sandys having made 'cuts' suggests that this type of lock must have been constructed even on the first Avon Navigation.

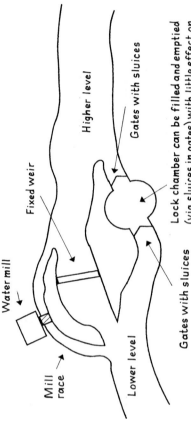

Higher level

Gates with sluices

Lock chamber can be filled and emptied (via sluices in gates) with little effect on level above weir. Gates may be opened for craft once water levels each side are equal.

Fixed weir

Water mill

Gates with sluices

Lower level

Mill race

A typical Avon water mill. Cropthorne Mill, one of the water mills now standing at Fladbury. The village boasted mills since the time of the Domesday book. *Author*

The mill and weir at Fladbury, Sandys' home village. The oldest parts of Fladbury Mill predate him. *Author*

corporation which says 'Mr William Sandes is to have the common seal to a petition . . . for assistance in his navigation . . .' Perhaps this help was to complete the works to allow year-round navigation to Stratford, perhaps for assistance for his projected improvements of its Arrow tributary, or perhaps it was for a Warwick extension.

Having worked so hard for the navigation, Sandys was to lose it again in a few years. Although the 1630s had been a good time for the Avon, they had been disastrous for the country as a whole. Charles I's rule was collapsing, and when in the early 1640s the Long Parliament used their new found powers to expel friends of the king, William Sandys was declared 'within the order made against monopolists, and not fit to sit as a member of this parliament'. The chickens of his probable bribes had come home to roost, and shortly after losing his seat, Sandys lost his river, being forced to give it up to William Say, a prominent anti-royalist, and apparently one of Sandys' original guarantors.

In Habingdon's account of the Navigation, recognition of Sandys difficulties (both in engineering and political terms) is given, and he concludes by saying:

[The River] will no doubt be established for this world's ever (if future ages suffer not by negligence so profittable a work to perish), and Mr William Sandys ever remembered as the founder thereof.

In fact, the river was almost allowed to perish only a few years afterwards, but until recent times Sandys had a monument. It was the custom of boatmen to refer to the old bollard on Cropthorne water-gate as 'Sandys' post'. No other memorial exists, except, of course, the river itself.

Cropthorne Water-gate, at the turn of the century. To the left of the gate itself, 'Sandys' Post' can be seen.
Charles Showell

Chapter Two

The River in the Civil War

Even with its unprecedented powers, the Parliament which had expelled Sandys from its body was unable to establish harmony between the People and Crown. Torn apart by disputes over royal hegemony and by religious bigotry, the nation divided into those supporting a puritan Parliamentary revolution, and those maintaining loyalty to their Catholic King. Even those who were for their own part indifferent to the outcome were forced to take sides by their masters and peers. In a last, desperate attempt to re-establish his hold over the country, Charles I raised an army and the Civil War began. Between 1642 and 1649, when England's fields played host to a series of bloody battles, its fledgeling industrial economy lost the stability necessary for its proper growth. A fairly minor casualty, in the context of the national upheaval taking place, was inland navigation.

During the period of fighting, the River Avon, whose banks had witnessed the collapse of Simon de Montfort's earlier attempt at revolution, and had shaped the last battle of the Wars of the Roses, reverted to its customary rôle as a strategic barrier to communication. Over the years of struggle its water, which had borne barges for the first time so recently, was to flow over new stony shallows where great bridges once stood, and the locks which had penned back its flow were to fall into disuse and neglect. While the local commercial ramifications of the Civil War are too complex to chart in detail, the direct physical blockages caused by army action are well recorded, and give a vivid impression of the extent to which ordinary life was disrupted by the struggles for political power.

Of the various bridges over the river, one of the most important was at Evesham, situated on the road between the two Royalist cities of Worcester and Oxford. Its position 'rendered early occupation by Royalists a matter of importance, without which communication between these cities...could not be effectively maintained'. In July 1642, the peace of this quiet market town was shattered by the arrival of the King's forces, who made it a fortified stronghold against the roundhead army. The Governor of the new garrison was Samuel Sandys, of the same family as William. In April 1643, the defences built by the royalist army (at considerable expense to the townspeople) were to prove very useful to Prince Maurice, who camped there for a few days during his retreat from a skirmish at Ripple Field. Five days later, Charles I himself used the garrison as a haven of retreat from his defeat at Cropredy Bridge. Leaving Evesham on Thursday 6th July, 1644, his retreating army destroyed its bridge to prevent the roundheads under Walker from pursuing them, and blocked the navigation with fallen masonry. Perhaps because of their treatment by the cavaliers, the townspeople were inclined to support the Parliamentarians, and they made temporary repairs to the bridge at once. Later, the King returned to fine the townspeople £200, and to knock their bridge down once again! Evesham was finally taken by the Cromwellian Colonel, Massey, in 1645.

Pershore Bridge, whose central arch exacted such a severe revenge on those who sought to destroy it during the civil war. Having borne its weight for hundreds of years, the bridge was relieved of the burden of main road traffic half a century ago when a modern concrete structure was built a few yards away. The difficulty of navigating these arches in times of high water is demonstrated vividly by the eddies in the current.

Author

Another crossing point on the river was at Pershore, whose bridge carried the London to Aberystwyth (thence Ireland) postal road. Royalist soldiers destroyed it in June 1644, but this was not without some difficulty, and when its central arch finally fell some 80 workmen were crushed and drowned. Even then, only that one arch was broken, though a week later the roundhead Walker managed to destroy it utterly. In Stratford upon Avon, the ancient Clopton Bridge was badly damaged, one arch being demolished. This was repaired to its original condition after the end of the wars. With the remains of so many fallen bridges blocking it, as well as neglect and lack of custom for its services, it is not surprising that during the Civil War the waterway fell into disuse.

When peace was restored, the new Parliament began the reconstruction of the nation's economy, and William Say was able to set about the restoration of his river. Facing him were 13 or 14 neglected locks and weirs, the heavy remains of fallen bridges, and the problems of a limited supply of capital. These difficulties notwithstanding, he is said to have 'completed' the first eight locks and weirs between Evesham and Tewkesbury within a short time. For traffic to have flowed before the war, the structures must have been in working order, so perhaps 'completed' in this context simply means restored. William Say also had to make his own arrangements for access to land, especially that which had been the subject of dispute in Sandys' time. For example Say and his partner (William Harte of Kent) agreed to lease for 2,000 years,

All that the sluce and late cutt watercourse with the appurtanances in or neare Nafford . . . and near to the mill there called Nafford Mill . . . and also parte of the sluce and late cutt watercourse . . . neare Strensham Mills . . . and likewise the line wayes though all theire . . . meadow grounds . . . as the same lyne ways are and have been used for drawing of boats and barges . . . in and through the sluces.

It is probable, in the light of information presented in the following chapter, that William Say's work never succeeded in rebuilding Sandys' river all the way to Stratford, and he may well have gone no further east than Evesham.

Although the proprietors of the Coventry coal-field, who were the principal intended beneficiaries of Sandys' original plans, would not have benefited from Say's river at all, the towns and villages along its banks were able to enjoy greater wealth brought by its trade. An excellent example is Wyre Piddle, a small waterside village between Evesham and Pershore, whose development has been studied by the local historian Catherine Hammond.

The increased prosperity in Wyre [after the reopening of the Avon] was reflected in the building or rebuilding of three large farmhouses at this period; Manor farm, Yew tree farm and Wyre House. . . The George Inn opened to cater for the needs of bow-haulers bringing their wares up the Avon. There would have been ample custom for the George Inn at this time.

The death of Cromwell, in 1658, precipitated another short period of instability, culminating in a national tax strike, dissolution of the Army, and finally free elections which restored King Charles II to the British Throne. Anxious to avoid further conflict between rival factions of the revolutionary years, the new monarch passed an 'Act of Indemnity and Oblivion' - essentially a pardon for those who had supported Cromwell's cause. The only men excepted from this Act were the regicides, who had actually signed the death warrant of his father. Among the names on that document was that of William Say. As part of his punishment, he lost all of his estate, including the Avon Navigation, which was granted to the trustees of the Duke of York in September 1661.

Under the new King, William Sandys was again able to stand for Parliament and he was re-elected in 1661. In the intervening years, he had clearly not tired of opening rivers, and returned to his original plan of making the Avon navigable all the way to Coventry, where he rented some mines. However, his application to purchase the river was not successful, and he was never again connected with the navigation he had built as a visionary young man.

Despite William's failure to regain possession of the Avon, the Sandys family name remained connected with other waterways. He had proposed to make the River Teme navigable at about the same time that he worked on the Avon. After his death, in 1662, his cousin Harry Sandys, and also Windsor Sandys, were appointed undertakers of the navigation of the Wye and Lug. They attempted to tame the wild Wye with the same types of lock which had been used on the Avon, with some degree of success. Also, in 1670, Windsor Sandys had rights in the Wey Navigation. The Avon went on to be a success, as did the Wey. The non-tidal Wye Navigation has fallen into ruin, and the river is now navigable only in winter floods, when it offers one of the most spectacular inland waterway journeys in Britain*.

A cargo-carrying sailing barge at Stratford on Avon (the spire of Holy Trinity Church can be seen to the left). The bowsprit sticking out ahead of the boat was presumably built to aid leverage when raising or lowering the mast.   *Stratford Record Office Collection*

---

* Using experience gained on the Avon, a group of waterways enthusiasts is currently planning restoration of the Wye to year-round navigability.

Chapter Three

Great Plans for a Small River

Although Sandys failed to regain the river from the Duke's trustees, it was bought two years later by his cousin Thomas, Lord Windsor, who had been one of the original 1635 commissioners. On 9th September, 1664 he granted part of the river to a syndicate consisting of Andrew Yarranton, Richard Hunt, Richard Bartlett, Richard Turton and Nicholas Baker. These men were to make navigable that part of the river that they owned, which extended from Bidford to Stratford, 'in such wise that the same shall carry a barge laden with Ten Tons at least from the said town of Stratford to the said town of Evesham'. The lightness of this load may reflect continuing difficulties in maintaining adequate depth in the dry season. To achieve this, the Upper Avon syndicate spent £600 of their own money, building six sluices. Presumably, these were at Sandys' old sites - Harvington lock, Cleeve Prior lock, Bidford water-gate, Grange lock, Welford lock and Luddington lock. The river below Evesham, which was already in full use, was retained by Windsor who was also to receive a toll of 4d. per ton on goods carried on the syndicate's Upper River once it was open.

The date of completion, 1666, is the third date which is given for the 'opening of the Avon Navigation'. Habingdon is clear that it was open in the early 1640s, and the same is implied elsewhere by authors who refer to it falling into disuse during the war. Other historians say it was completed by William Say, and yet others that it was completed in 1666. The accounts are contradictory, and the best explanation seems to be as follows. Habingdon was correct, and the river was open for at least part of the year throughout, by the 1640s. It was probably not completed for year-round navigation. The Civil War destroyed it, and part (to Evesham) was rebuilt by Say. The reconstruction of the part of the river above Evesham had to wait for the the 1664 syndicate. At least after this time, all sources agree that the river was open and in use, and in 1677 coal from Madley (Severn-side) was being sold at 7s. 6d. per ton at Bidford wharf. There is even a hint that the reaches between Stratford and Warwick were again being used for light craft; one Thomas Smith was indicted in 1669 for blocking the navigation channel at Barford.

Although the syndicate was led largely by Richard Bartlett, the most interesting of its members from an historian's point of view was Andrew Yarranton, 'The founder of English political economy'. Yarranton was born in 1619 in Larford in the parish of Astly, and in his sixteenth year he was apprenticed to a linen draper. He continued in that trade for a few years, but then he left, the shop being in his words 'too narrow and short for my large mind'. He then lived as a countryman for several years before becoming a captain of the Roundhead army. In 1652 he started working in the iron industry. A relic of this time of his life was uncovered on 31st May, 1924, when a flood broke the dam at Sharply Pool, an ornamental lake in Glasshampton (Astly), to reveal the remains of one of his furnaces. He also became interested in Navigation, and made Dick Brook (a tributary of the Severn) passable for small boats in 1652.

His ambition increasing, Captain Yarranton considered using his Dick Brook experience for creating many new navigations. He recalled:

> I made it my business to survey the three great rivers of England [Thames, Severn and Humber] and some small ones, and made two navigable [Worcestershire Stour and Avon] and a third almost complete [Salwarpe].

Interestingly, Lord Windsor was involved in the work on the Salwarpe and the (Worcestershire) Stour.

During his time in ironworking, Yarranton had obviously been thinking about the state of British industry as a whole, and comparing it to that of other countries in Europe, especially Holland, with whom England was then at war (Dutch ships had managed to invade Kentish rivers at the height of this conflict). According to his biographer, P.E. Dove, his analysis made him

> . . . the first man in England who saw that peace was better than war, that trade was better than plunder, that honest industry was better than material greatness, and that the best occupation of a government was to secure property at home and let other nations alone.

The outcome of this study was a book, published in 1676, called 'England's Improvement by Sea and Land', and subtitled 'to out-do the Dutch without fighting'. The book was dedicated to Thomas, Lord Windsor, who was connected with many of his commercial ventures.

After an analysis of Dutch ways, gathered during a visit to Holland, Yarranton proceeded to suggest that it would be impossible to beat them by force, and said that improving England would be a far better use of resources. In a chapter headed 'The way to employ and set to work all the poor of England, both Man and Woman and child that are capable and able to work, and all to be done by improving two of our own manufactures . . . the one linen and the other iron manufacture', he set up a strategy. England didn't produce much linen or flax, and had to import them at a high price. Holland and Flanders, however, made large amounts of linen from flax brought down from Germany by way of the Rhine and Elbe. Yarranton suggested that by producing her own linen, England could stop buying Dutch produce and even compete with Holland for foreign markets.

> Is it not pity and shame, that the young children and maids here in England should be idle within doors, begging abroad, tearing hedges or robbing orchards, and worse, when these, and these alone, are the people that may, and must if ever, set up this trade of making linen here?

In selecting a place to start the proposed Industry, he said,

> Warwick, Leicester, Northampton and Oxfordshires are the places to set up this manufacture, because in these counties there is at present no staple trade, and the land there for flax is very good, being rich and dry, wherein flax doth abundantly delight. . . . their poor and idle want imployment.

After so many years, it is difficult to judge how altruistic were Yarranton's proposals for what would now be called 'job creation'. He may have been genuinely concerned to provide employment in especially deprived areas, or he may have realised that these are precisely the places at which the cheapest labour force might be found. Whatever his real motive, he selected Milcote Manor near Stratford-upon-Avon, to be an excellent place for Flax production.

> If the whole mannor were soen with Flax, it would imploy nine thousand people in the manufacturing thereof, as to sowing, weeding, pulling, watering, dressing, spinning, winding, weaving and whitening . . . The Flax and thereall being *carried down the river Avon* into Severne and so conveyed with ease to Bristol, Wales and other parts, to set the poor at work which want employment . . .[my emphasis]

The quality of water was thought to be important for making good flax, and Yarranton said that he knew two places in England where suitable water was at hand; Stratford-upon-Avon and Coventry. In the first place, he suggested setting up a New Town near Stratford, on the banks of the river, to be called 'New Haarlem' after the Dutch Flax processing town. The exact site was to be at Upper Milcote, just downstream of Stratford, where the Avon and Stour met.

In the next part of 'England's improvement by Sea and Land', its author discusses corn for both food and mum, a beer-like beverage. During poor years for agriculture, food supply in England was erratic and there was no cheap distribution system to help needy areas. Again, drawing from his experiences of Europe, Yarranton described the granaries of Magdenburgh;

> . . . wherein corn is kept sweet and safe from vermin. . . . From hence the Brunswick people fetch their wheat they make mum of; and down the Elbe to Hamborough is sent infinite of corn out of the granaries; amd from there to all parts that stand in need thereof.

He went on to suggest that a set of granaries ahould be set up to store corn for emergency use, at Wellinborough, King's Mill (Leics), Banbury, Lechlade and Stratford-upon-Avon. Each of these places is of course on a river (Nene, Soar, Cherwell, Thames and Avon respectively) although not all were navigable then. Again, the Stratford site is discussed in detail;

> Stratford-on-Avon . . . will be a very good place to build granaries to receive corn; and I will affirm, if there be three or four large granaries built in the lands of Sir John Clapton [Clopton] near the bridge at Stratford, and well managed for the good of the poor, and linen trade; that on that side of the river there would be in a very short time as great a town as Stratford now is; and there have as great a trade as any city in these parts of England (Bristol only excepted).

He suggested calling the new town 'New Brunswick', and appealed in the book to his friend Mr Bishop, the Town Clerk, to help him set up a mum trade. He closes the section with an address to the people of the area:

> Now all improvements offer themselves to you; as the mum trade, the linen and thread trade . . . you will be to the West of England . . . as Dantzick is to Poland; you will serve

all these parts when corn is wanting; you have the advantage of your Navigable River to send down your corn, and so by the Severn it will be carried into all parts that stand in need thereof.

The Ordnance Survey map on page 85 shows Bridgetown which stands near the proposed site for Yarranton's industrial new town, New Brunswick.

Had these plans come to fruition, the trade on the river would have been very large indeed, as Yarranton predicted: he would have recouped his outlay on the Avon many times over. The next plan of his, had it been realised, would have made even this traffic seem small. Passage from the east to the west of England could only be done by land or, for larger cargoes, by sea. The sea passage could become hazardous in winter, and also dangerous for strategic reasons. The burning of English ships by the Dutch in Chatham harbour was a vivid illustration of the latter point. What was needed was an inland waterway, linking the Thames and the Severn, and Yarranton proposed such a route. He acknowledged previous proposals, such as that of Francis Matthew who suggested linking the Warwickshire Avon to the Welland, which had been judged impractical. Yarranton believed he had a workable scheme, writing;

. . . this summer my Son hath twice surveyed the river Thames and Charwell, and it is very evident that the Charwell may be made Navigable to Banbury, and the river Stower [Stour] from Shipton [Shipston] clear into Avon near Stratford. So there will be a communication of the two great rivers for water carriage within eight miles. And that eight miles for land Carriage will be of good hilly found dry land' [The distance between Banbury and Shipston is actually nearly 15 miles by road].

He estimated that the making navigable of the Stour would cost £4,000, and the Cherwell £10,000. The junction of the rivers Avon and Stour would have been, of course, the proposed site for New Haarlem, allowing the town trade to both east and westwards.

Alas for Yarranton, his great plans failed to inspire those with the power and money to make them reality, and far from being the centre of a new industrial revolution the town was to change little in character from the one Shakespeare knew. The Cherwell was never made truly navigable, the approximate route being opened only when Brindley's Oxford Canal was built many years later. The (Warwickshire) Stour Navigation came to nothing, and the way was eventually opened by a canal-owned tramway (see later). With the exception of the Avon, the navigations which Yarranton did manage to build fell into ruin. The Worcestershire Stour was navigable to Stourbridge in 1677, but was destroyed in less than a decade, by a combination of floods and vandalism - Brindley's Staffordshire and Worcestershire Canal now runs beside its remains. The Salwarpe, which may never have been truly navigable, was replaced by the Droitwich Barge Canal.

Even without Yarranton's proposed engineering of the local economy, trade on the Avon was still vigorous enough to justify its upkeep, and the syndicate continued to make improvements. Once the river was made fully navigable up to Stratford, Lord Windsor split the Upper Avon into 15 shares, and re-purchased two of these himself, giving a total of $\frac{7}{15}$ owned by him and $\frac{8}{15}$ owned by the syndicate. Yarranton complained of this forced change, in his book. A new member, by the name of John Woodin, joined the syndicate during the period of rebuiliding, and later bought more of the shares.

Andrew Yarranton's idealistic book notwithstanding, England was still at war with Holland, and the Navy was impressing (conscripting) water-men of all kinds to serve in its ranks. In May 1672, Yarranton petitioned Parliament for exemption for his men from being conscripted. In his plea, he described himself as 'owner of the greatest part of the said Navigation . . . He having adventured his whole estate on that work'. His petition succeeded, with exemption being given for 68 men, the crews of 22 barges. This figure gives some idea of the volume of trade at the time.

Inland Navigation in Yarranton's Time

Detail of a drawing showing a sailing barge by Clopton Bridge, Stratford. The activities of the crew suggest that the craft is docking rather than leaving, and that the barrels and millstones are therefore to be loaded for export from the town.

Stratford Record Office Collection

A cargo boat downstream of Pershore Bridge.   *Almonry Museum*

Chapter Four

Years of Prosperity

The late 17th and early 18th centuries were to lead to a time of comparive prosperity for the proprietors of the Avon. There were some local difficulties, especially during the recession of the 1670s when 'Mobs of the poorer sort of people' were breaking into mills to seize corn, and vandalising lockgear. Justices of the peace bound over several offenders at Quarter Sessions, but after John Woodin reported that the offenders had 'humbled themselves' and given undertakings that they would behave well in the future, the Privy Council dropped the case. These minor disturbances were not serious enough to prevent growth in river traffic, and Woodin leased river-side land for use as a large coal yard in the grounds of Sir John Clopton at the head of navigation in Stratford. The traffic heading furhter upstream was even intense enough for towing ropes to cause a frequent nuisance to horses crossing Clopton's Bridge.

Movement of coal constituted much of the river's traffic, but its direction was opposite to that intended by Sandys. His original design would have allowed Midlands coal to be exported downstream to the South-West, whereas the actual flow was towards Warwickshire from the mines of Severnside (Broseley/Ironbridge region, between Bridgnorth and Shrewsbury). Madeley collieries, for example, exported coal to Bidford where it was sold at 7s. 6d. per ton in 1677. As well as this staple mineral traffic, the Navigation provided a means of transport for other wares, for industry, food manufacture and for merchants of luxury goods. Daniel Defoe, visiting Stratford in 1725, illustrates clearly the benefits of this ready route for import and export to the valley's economy:

[The river is] An exceeding advantage to all this part of the country and also to the commerce of the City of Bristol. For by this river they derive a very great trade for sugar, oil, wine, tobacco, iron, lead and in a word, all heavy goods which are carried by water almost as far as Warwick; and in return the corn, and especially the cheese, is brought back from Gloucestershire and Warwickshire to Bristol.

In connection with his mention of tobacco, it is interesting that two records, of 1682 and 1737, both mention the presence of several tobacconists in Stratford.

When Lord Windsor died, in 1687, his rights to the river passed to his second wife, Ursula. In a submission to the House of Commons in 1695, she valued her revenue from coal traffic to be some £400 a year. This large sum was not, of course, simply obtained by the practice of charging tolls to carrying companies, as became the practice in the 'canal age'. The river owned by Ursula Windsor still worked according to Sandy's Act, and there was no general right of navigation. As with the railway practice which evolved with the coming of steam, the owner of the transport route could be its major or only carrier, or could sub-contract the work as necessary. A coal tax, imposed in 1695, made a temporary dent in business, but within nine years traffic was sufficiently large

A cargo boat at Strensham.   *Charles Showell*

Transporting reeds was free of tolls under the 1751 Act, a concession useful to those involved in supplying the thatching, basket-making and matting trades. Behind this small punt is Strensham Mill, which was destroyed by fire in 1958 (four Avon mills have been lost in fires this century).   *J. Garrett*

for a Pershore merchant, Mark Ramell, to wish to lease the river below Evesham. He was granted a 21-year lease. for the sum of £328 per year, from 11th October, 1704. The arrangement gave him the rights to carry Shropshire, Staffordshire and Worcestershire coal (all brought down the Severn) and all kinds of goods to Evesham and Pershore, and also to take the profits from Pershore Sluice. The Upper Avon Syndicate continued to run their part of the river, serving Bidford and Stratford, but their vessels would have to pay Rammell's toll at Pershore.

When Ursula Windsor, Countess of Plymouth, died in 1717, the split ownership of the navigation was perpetuated, being divided between her sons Andrew and Thomas, who inherited the stretches above and below Evesham respectively. Since that day, the river has never been under the control of a single owner. A few years later, in 1738, Thomas died and his son, Herbert, took over the lower river.

Now that it was carrying such a large traffic, the old operating arrangements were proving unsatisfactory. The owners' total control gave them a free hand to set the price of goods brought up by their sub-contracting boatmen, which was a source of annoyance both to their immediate customers and to the final customers to whom the costs were passed. Barge-masters also suffered the expense of paying millers for the privilege of passing their weirs, the cost being particularly exhorbitant when the river was low, or the cargo perishable. Theoretically, Sandys' arrangements allowed for the settling of such grievances by the commissioners, but they had, of course, died long ago, so there was no regulatory body save Parliament itself. When the problems of the busy river were brought to Westminster, they were solved by the passing of an Act, effective from September 1751:

An Act for the better regulating of the Navigation of the River Avon, running through the counties of Warwick, Worcester, and Gloucester; and for ascertaining the Rates of Water Carriage upon the said river.

During the preamble, the paper talks of

Boats, barges, lighters and other vessels . . . with Pit coal, Iron and other goods . . . for the publick good of the said counties, whereby the trade in these parts hath been very much inlarged and magnified,

again recognising the beneficial effect of the Navigation on the area. The purpose of Parliamentary action was stated to be settlement of disputes between 'Owners and proprietors of the Said Navigation and those navigating thereupon'.

The 1751 Act stated that the Avon would become a 'Free River', and 'all and every person and persons shall have liberty of passing up and down the said river'. Thus the proprietors lost their monopoly over carriage, and the system which came to be used on later waterways was applied. Recognising the conflicting interests of the bargemen and millers, Parliament set a legal fee - 'Millers must draw water for money not exceeding 1s. 3d. per mill, within one hour of the request' - and compelled them to be prepared to drain a reach of

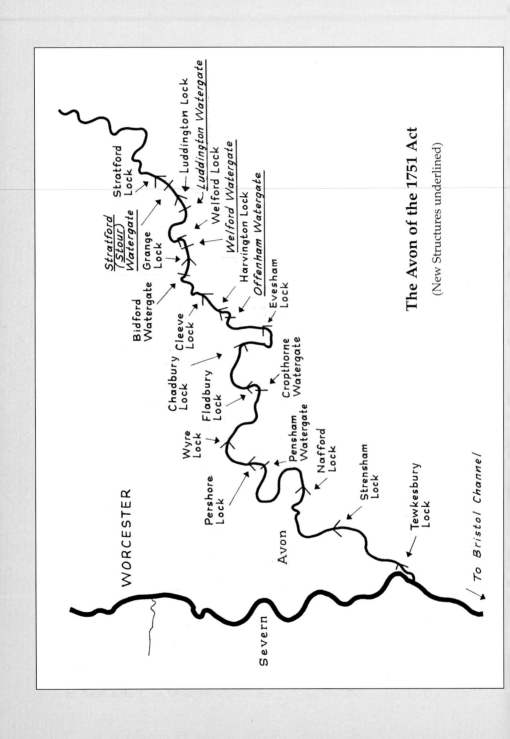

WORCESTER

Severn

Avon

Pershore
Lock

Wyre
Lock

Pensham
Watergate

Nafford
Lock

Strensham
Lock

Tewkesbury
Lock

To Bristol Channel

Fladbury
Lock

Cropthorne
Watergate

Chadbury
Lock

Cleeve
Lock

Bidford
Watergate

Evesham
Lock

Offenham Watergate

Harvington Lock

Welford Watergate

Welford Lock

Luddington Watergate

Luddington Lock

Grange
Lock

*Stratford
(Stour)
Watergate*

Stratford
Lock

The Avon of the 1751 Act

(New Structures underlined)

river for maintenance works at 24 hours notice. Tolls for the passage of goods
were fixed in the act, as below:

Goods	Rate	Goods	Rate
Wine	4s./ton	Clover	3s./ton
Cyder	4s./ton	Meal	3s./ton
Merchants' goods	4s./ton	Pig Iron	10d./ton
Wheat	3s./Wey	Brick	10d./ton
Barley	3s./Wey	Stone	10d./ton
Malt	3s./Wey	Lime	10d./ton
Beans	3s./Wey	Timber	10d./ton
Date	3s./Wey	Wood	10d./ton
Linseed	3s./Wey	Coal and other	1s. 6d./ton
Flour	3s./Wey		

This list can, presumably, be assumed to cover all of the major categories of
freight carried at the time. Mineral-carrying boats were to have their draughts
painted on the side of their hulls, as commonly practised today, to eliminate
disputes over actual tonnages.

The duties of bargemasters to pay these tolls could be enforced under the Act;
the proprietors would able to seize the boat and goods of a debtor, and if
necessary sell them to recover their fee. Similarly, the duty of lock-keepers was
assured by the provision of a severe fine (40 shillings) which would be imposed
on any who refused to assist the passage of a barge through his lock. The same
fine was payable by any waterman who obstructed others on the river, and any
damage done by a boat was the responsibility of its master, as was the conduct
of his crew. It was made very clear that

> No bargeman or other person shall, at any time whatsoever, draw any floodgates of any
> dams, or lashers of any sluice, or set or leave any weir, without the consent of the
> owners.

For their part, the proprietors were required to keep the works of the
Navigation in good repair. Concessions were given to riparian owners,
allowing farmers to transport reeds and compost without charge, and pleasure
boats were allowed to be used freely. First made fashionable by the yachting
monarch Charles II, pleasure boating was not, of course, the popular activity it
has become this century, but neither was it completely unknown - several
gentlemen of the time delighted in undertaking small 'adventures' by water,
and some of the comments of those who 'cruised' the Avon, such as Taylor,
have been quoted in the pages of this book. Because of the split ownership of
the River, it was stated that no public wharf could be built between Evesham
and Harvington, that is between the top lock on the Lower river and the bottom
on the Upper. This would prevent bargemasters cheating on tolls. The Act
concluded:

> In case of any difficulties, disputes or differences shall hereafter arise ... it shall and
> may be lawful for any two or more of His Majesty's Justices of the Peace ... to issue their
> warrant ... to hear and determine ... in a summary way ... and to award damages

In the preamble, the navigation was described; there were 14 pound locks, at Tewkesbury, Strensham, Nafford, Pershore, Fladbury, Chadbury, Evesham, Harvington, Cleeve, Bidford Grange, Welford, Luddington and Stratford-upon-Avon. In addition to these, there were six water-gates, at Pensham, Cropthorne, Harvington, Bidford, Welford, Luddington and Stratford (*see map page 34*). Three years after the Act came into force, Herbert Lord Windsor leased the Lower Avon to an Evesham man, Joseph Biddle. The rent was £630 per annum for the same rights as Mark Rammell. The increase in rent, from £328 to £630, reflects the increase in profitability of the river under its new rules.

In its purely physical aspects, navigation of the Avon had changed little. Contemporary sketches of the boats, a few of which are reproduced in these pages, show several types of a basically similar design. Most were of 30-40 feet in length, and powered by a single square sail set on a mast, which must have been pivoted for negotiation of bridges. Some appear to be flat-transomed, while others have more curved sterns. Steering was either by a long oar or, especially on the larger vessels, by a proper rudder. The addition of new water-gates to the Upper Avon (Harvington, Welford, Luddington and Stratford) must have resulted in considerable improvement in the available depth, allowing the use of larger boats, more heavily loaded than in the preceding century. Sailing the Avon is difficult, even with today's smooth hulls and Bermudan-Rig sails, because the prevailing winds are not strong, and because the river meanders so. With the comparatively crude barges of the 18th century, sailing all the way up river in a reasonable time would not have been feasible. The Avon has never had a horse tow-path, so the barges would still have to be hauled much of the way by the crew or by hired 'bow-hauliers'. These men would pull the boat by means of a long rope, usually attached to the top of the mast so that it would pass over trees and not pull the bows too close to the bank. The 'bow' in 'bow-haulier' refers not to the front of a boat, incidentally, but to the bows tied in the rope on which they pulled - it is therefore pronounced to rhyme with crow (or trow!). This type of haulage, which the great engineer Telford was later to call 'The barbarous . . . and expensive custom of performing this slave-like office by men' brought in good custom for the local hostelries. At Wyre Piddle, the 'George' added yet another room!

The most serious obstructions to bow-hauling were bridges, which necessitated lowering of the vessel's mast, thus depriving it of wind power. Downstream craft could simply drift through with the current, using a long shaft of wood to keep them off the masonry, but those bound upstream required a more complicted procedure. While the boat was being held just downstream of the bridge, a coil of rope would be carried up on to the bridge. Then, a log would be tied to one of its ends and dropped over the upstream parapet, the other end being firmly held by the crewman on the bridge. When the log had floated down to the waiting boat, the new rope, which passed through the arch, would replace the previous one, and the boat could be pulled through. Soft sandstone bridges such as the one at Pershore had deep trenches cut into them by the ropes, and even today one can inspect these mute memorials of the toil of men long ago. Sir Arthur Quiller-Couch found inspiration for one of his most famous poems in the marks on Eckington bridge, which crosses the Avon between Pershore and Tewkesbury;

> Man shall outlast his battles. They have swept
> Avon from Naseby Field to Severn Ham;
> And Evesham's dedicated stones have stepp'd
> Down to the dust with Montfort's oriflamme.
> Nor the red tear nor the reflected tower
> Abides; but yet these eloquent grooves remain,
> Worn in the sandstone parapet hour by hour
> By labouring bargemen where they shifted ropes.
> E'en so shall man turn back from violent hopes
> To Adam's cheer, and toil with spade again.

While the changing fortunes of the river's proprietors are recorded in County Record Offices, little is known about the lives of boatmen.   No specific references to Avon sailors seem to exist, and study of comments made on the lot of boatmen on other rivers makes it hard to generalise.   For example, on the Medway in 1600 it was said that a boatman 'doth labour very ill yf his dayes worke be not worth him xvi*d*. [about 7 new pence]'.   Later, in 1671, a toll of 1*d*./ton was put on coal to help out the 'poverty of the bargemen, their families and others occasioned by the navigation'.   However, in 1712 a Guildford bargemaster (the River Wey) could afford to apprentice his two sons for £43. From these accounts, covering comparative richness and real poverty, it is impossible to build up any general picture over the country or period.   As so often happens in history, those who laboured so hard for the wealth of their masters were forgotten in the records of their writing contemporaries.

Deep grooves in the soft stone of Pershore Bridge, left by ropes of generations of Avon boatmen.   *Author*

Jonathan Hulls' Tug (an illustration from his pamphlet).

Ecklington Bridge, the stones of which inspired Quiller Couch's poem quoted in the text. These many-arched bridges are common along the Avon, examples being found at Tewkesbury, Eckington, Pershore, Bidford and Stratford. Before it was rebuilt last century, Evesham's bridge was also of this type. *Author*

Chapter Five

The World's First Steamboat

During their long history, Avon's waters have been associated with many heroic failures. Simon de Montfort, the Earl of Leicester who fought for greater Parliamentary government, fell at Evesham, trapped by a loop of the river. Two of Andrew Yarranton's schemes for improving the country had involved the Avon, both as a Thames-Severn link and a site for industrial New Towns. Much later in the river's story are instances when small groups of individuals made heroic stands against rich and powerful opponents and lost. However, one of the its most unusual tales concerns the almost forgotten figure of a Gloucestershire farmer with a passion for mechanics, Jonathan Hulls.

Hulls was born in the year 1699, in the Gloucester village of Hanging Aston (now called Aston Magna). During his education at the nearby Chipping Campden Grammar School, he developed a keen interest in mechanics and became a part-time clock repairer. By the age of 19, when he got married, he was able to use his earnings to purchase 60 acres of premium land at Broad Campden, and also horses to keep on it. His interest in engineering continued to flourish, it seems, because in 1736 he was ready to patent an invention using Newcommen's recently-invented atmospheric engine to power a water-borne vessel. Having received capital support of £160 from a Mr Freeman of Batsford Park, Hulls applied to Queen Caroline for a patent (George II being away in Hannover at this time). Letters Patent were granted for 14 years, subject to the condition that a full specification be filed within three months, the patent being dated 21st December, 1736.

In March 1737, Hulls published his description of the boat, entitled 'A Description and Draught of a New Invented Machine for Conveying Vessels or Ships out of or into any Harbour, Port or River, Against Wind and Tide or in a Calm'. The illustration of the craft is reproduced opposite. Having realised that the engine would be somewhat bulky and expensive, he suggested that it should be mounted in a special boat (which we would nowadays call a tug) which could be used to tow a variety of conventional craft. On the subject of the size and power of the machinery, Hulls assured the reader:

Note - The bigness of the machines may be proportioned to the work that is to be performed by them; but if such a force as is applied in this first essay be not sufficient for any purpose that may be required, there is room to make such addition as will move an immense weight with tolerable swiftness.

Fortunately for historians, the pamphlet described the minutiae of the machinery in great detail; the salient points are set out below.

The engine itself was simply a Newcommen type, equipped with a boiler ('a vessel about two thirds full of water, with the top close shut'), and a closed cylinder, one end of which was formed by a moveable piston. The boiler generated steam at low pressure, and outward movement of the piston sucked

Hulls' Mechanism

Proportions have been altered to show mechanism more clearly. All connections to axles other than the two labelled ratchets are rigid. Links to operate steam and injector valves automatically have been omitted in the interests of clarity.

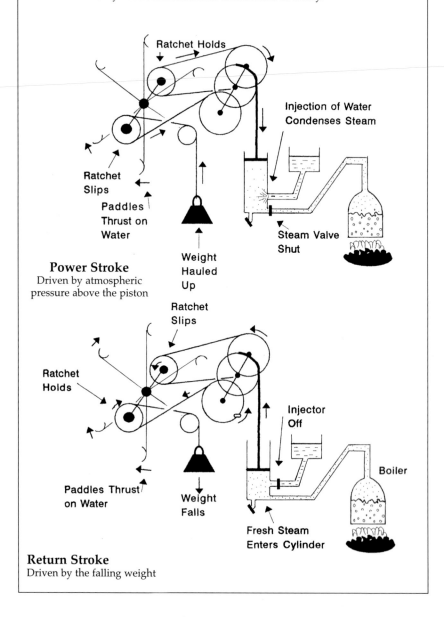

Ratchet Holds

Injection of Water
Condenses Steam

Ratchet
Slips

Paddles
Thrust on
Water

Steam Valve
Shut

Weight
Hauled
Up

Power Stroke
Driven by atmospheric
pressure above the piston

Ratchet
Slips

Ratchet
Holds

Injector
Off

Paddles Thrust
on Water

Weight
Falls

Boiler

Fresh Steam
Enters Cylinder

Return Stroke
Driven by the falling weight

this into the cylinder through a valve, which shut as soon as the piston reached the end of its travel. The steam in the cylinder was then sprayed with cold water through another valve, so that it condensed, thus creating a partial vacuum. The difference in pressure between the inside of the cylinder and the air outside caused the piston to rush inwards with great force; this force was transmitted to the boat's paddle gear by an absurdly complicated system of wheels, ropes, weights and ratchets, which also controlled the openings and closings of the engine's steam valves. The working of Hulls' unusual mechanism is illustrated opposite.

The elaborate arrangement of parts for transforming oscillatory to rotative motion, reminiscent of the devices immortalised by the late Heath Robinson, was, of course, unduly complicated. A simple crank would have performed much better, but in Hulls' time the device was not used in steam engineering and several other arrangements were tried before the patenting of the crank, by Boulton and Watt. Interestingly, Hulls suggested a modification of his mechanism for inland navigation:

> Up in-land rivers, where the bottom can possibly be reached, the fans [paddles] may be taken out, and cranks placed at the hindmost axis to strike a shaft to the bottom of the river, which will drive the vessel with greater force.

Thus the first (and only?) mechanical punt was invented!

Having established his patent, Mr Hulls may have set about building a prototype. One author, K.T. Rowland, clearly says he did, the engine itself being produced at the Eagle foundry in Birmingham, and the boat being made in Evesham. In 1737, before a crowd of excited onlookers, Jonathan Hulls was said to have tested his boat on the waters of the Lower Avon at Evesham. Unfortunately (though not surprisingly) it failed, and the project collapsed. It is not even certain that it reached the prototype stage, as no other references to the machine mention a full-scale trial, and the records of the Birmingham Museum of Science and Industry and the Newcommen Society state that the Eagle Foundry did not exist in Hulls' time, being built in 1775 by Francis, Smith and Dearman. Whether or not the boat was built, the slow and low powered engines then available, together with the inefficient paddle arrangement used to move the boat, made the idea of a working and useful tug impractical to realise.

In the introduction to his 1737 pamphlet, Hulls had anticipated a certain amount of ridicule:

> There is one hardship lies too commonly upon those who propose to advance some new, though useful scheme for public benefit: the world abounding more in rash censure than in candid and unprejudiced estimation of things, if a person does not answer their expectation in every point . . . he too often meets with ridicule and contempt.

This was indeed his fate. An example of the ridicule, in the form of a school-child's chant, is given in Whitfield's *History of Chipping Campden*:

Jonathan Hull
With his paper skull
Tried to make a machine
To go 'gainst wind and stream
But he, like an ass
Couldn't bring it to pass
So at last was ashamed to be seen (Trad. Anon.)

(Whitfield suggests that the paper skull is a mechanic's cap.)

In the course of time, the idea of a steam boat did come to pass, and Hull's is not totally forgotten. The State Room of the *Queen Mary*, one of the great ships of Cunard Lines, was graced by his portrait - a fitting tribute to an inventor who thought far ahead of his time.

Perrott House in Pershore's main street, home to its builder, George Perrott from 1775.
Author

Chapter Six

The Canal Age and the Perrott Dynasty

Though they were still hauled by the efforts of men, rather than steam, Avon barges continued to ply a useful trade. In 1758, Herbert Lord Windsor died and his estate fell into Chancery; on 20th December, 1759 the Court offered the Lower Avon for sale. It was bought by Joshua Poole, an agent acting for a Yorkshire-born London lawyer, George Perrott.

Biddle's lease on the lower river expired the same year, and Perrott prefered looking after the river himself to re-letting it. Biddle had assured him that all of the locks were in good order, but the impression gained by their new owner as he inspected them was entirely different. In his own words, the works were in 'Ruin and Decay in so much that before and immediately after the expiration of the said lease the Navigation was entirely stoppt in many parts of the River.'

Perrott clearly considered that the waterway was well worth saving, and spent £4,000 on repairs. Its reopening was advertised in the 15th August, 1764 edition of *Aris's Birmingham Gazette*. An interesting hint of the rather unconventional approach taken in maintenance of the river comes from the Upper Avon at about this time. In his *Picturesque views on the Avon*, published in 1795, Samuel Ireland says,

> About two miles below Salford is Harvington Lock and weir, which has been repaired with some of the fragments, and it is said, even the statues from Evesham Abbey.

In defence of the proprietors, it should be noted that this Samuel Ireland was almost certainly the source of the more outrageous Shakespeare drinking myths, and his word on the matter should not be taken as conclusive!

Even when carriage started on the refurbished river, it was to suffer further difficulties. During the 1760s there were several riots over the Kingdom due to the high price of food, which rose and fell in value while wages remained relatively constant. These spread to the Avon;

> . . . several hundred persons, chiefly women and children, assembled in the neighbourhood of Pershore, in order to intercept and pillage some vessels, laden with corn and meal, that were going down the River Avon; Notice of which being sent to the Commanding Officer of the Dragoons stationed in this city [Worcester], desiring a military aid, a party of them marched that day to Pershore, and a Justice of the Peace being likewise applied to, he also attended and causing the Riot Act to be read, the Mob thought proper to disperse, without committing any violence.

Rioters and vandals committing damage to Navigations were in fact in great danger from the law. An Act of 1727 (1 Geo.II cap. 19) had made willful damage to river locks and other equipment punishable by three months imprisonment and public whipping, and a later Act (5 Geo.II cap. 33) increased this penalty to seven years transportation. Later still, the penalty became 'Death without clergy'! (8 Geo.II cap. 20).

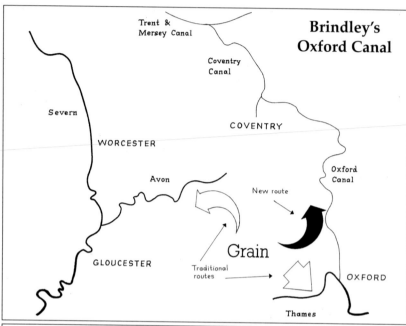

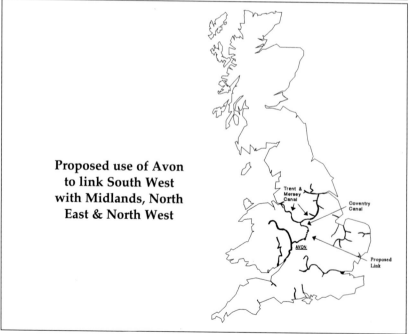

**Proposed use of Avon
to link South West
with Midlands, North
East & North West**

A threat to profit more serious than that from riots was competition from the new transport routes, which were beginning to have a major impact on British commerce. The first Turnpike Act (for the Great North Road) took effect in 1663, and gradually the new roads spread across the country. In 1728 the Act for the Evesham to Worcester turnpike was obtained (1 Geo.II cap. 11), competing with the river for Evesham to Pershore traffic especially, and also with goods travelling from Evesham to Worcester via the Avon and Severn. Slightly offsetting the deleterious effects of this competition were turnpikes which served the river's interests, such as that between Stratford and Long Compton (1730 - 3 Geo.II cap. 9), or Stratford and Alcester (1754 - 27 Geo.II cap.16), bringing these places into easy reach of the upper river.

Meanwhile, in the north of the country, the works of James Brindley began an even more significant transport revolution, which has come to be known as the 'canal age'. From fairly local affairs in the Liverpool and Manchester areas, interest in wholly artificial waterways grew, and in 1769, plans were published for a 'cut' linking the Thames markets with the mineral and industrial wealth of the Midlands. The Oxford Canal, engineered by James Brindley, would follow the Cherwell valley from Oxford to Cropredy, continue north-north-east to Rugby, turn west along the upper Avon valley for a few miles, and then go west-north-west towards Coventry (*opposite*). Hitherto, the productive cerial farms of Oxfordshire had sent long-distance exports in two directions - to London via the Thames, and to the South West via the rivers Avon and Severn. Coal and other minerals passed in the reverse direction. The proposed Oxford Canal would provide a new, easy route to the quickly-expanding markets of Midland industrial towns, leaving far less to travel by the old rivers with their floods, shoals and poor tow-paths. Fighting for the survival of his waterway, George Perrott petitioned Parliament against the Bill, explaining this;

> . . . divers large quantities of Coals were brought up the said River Avon and landed at Evesham and Stratford upon Avon . . . great part thereof were afterwards conveyed to, and sold at, Oxford, Chipping Norton, Woodstock, and divers other places, in the County of Oxford; and great quantities of corn and grain were brought from the County of Oxford, to Evesham and Stratford upon Avon . . . and there, and at other Mills upon the said River, ground into flour, and sent down the said River, to Bristol, and other places up and down the Severn, and other part of the said grain was sent down the said river unground, to the same places; and divers quantities of other goods were carried up and down the said river.

Perrott's attempt to prevent the building of the Oxford Canal was unsuccessful, but in the event he did not live long enough to see the new waterway completed. In the twilight of his life, he built a large riverside house in Pershore, and moved there after retiring from the Bench in 1775. The next year, he died, his memorial in Fladbury Church saying of him that 'his social and other amaible qualities rendered him beloved by all that knew him'. Under the terms of his Will, the Lower Avon passed to his nephew and namesake. Even the younger George Perrott was spared the effects of the Oxford Canal for many years - difficulties with its construction meant that it was 1790 before it was at last complete.

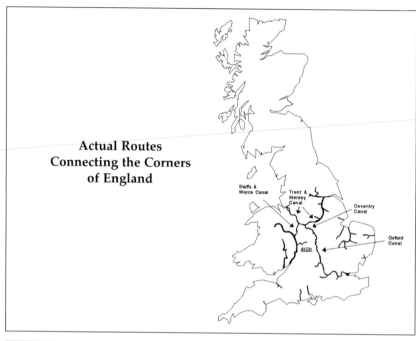

Actual Routes Connecting the Corners of England

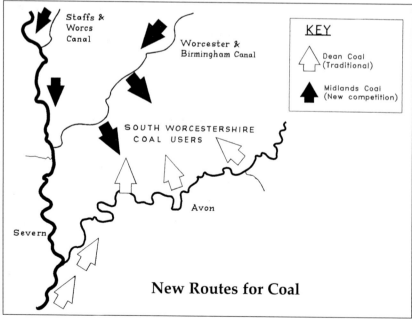

New Routes for Coal

While Perrott had total control of the lower river, the stretch above Evesham was in the hands of a consortium, whose members changed frequently. Shortly after the death of Herbert Lord Windsor, Mr Biddle, who had leased the Lower Avon before it passed to Perrott the elder, acquired a majority of shares in the Upper Avon. From 1766, the year that Biddle died, the majority holding passed to a local man, Thomas Ramell. Throughout this period, the river seems to have been improved steadily, by dredging and scouring, to enable it to carry vessels of greater burden.

Having seen the first wave of canal building taking place in the 1760s, the tradesmen of Statford-upon-Avon wondered whether their town could be joined to the main Midland canal network. At a meeting in Warwick in 1767, held in support of the proposal for the Coventry Canal, it was agreed that a possible line from Coventry to Warwick to join an extended Avon Navigation should surveyed. In a scheme every bit as bold as that of Yarranton, this would have created a Trent-Severn trunk route across England, avoiding the high lands around Birmingham (*see map page 44*). As related previously, the alternative scheme, joining the Coventry Canal to the Oxford Canal (and hence to the Thames and London - *see page 46*), won the day.

Later, in April 1774, when the waterway which is nowadays called the Grand Union Canal (Birmingham to London, passing through Leamington Spa near Warwick) was first discussed, a suggestion appeared in *Aris's Birmingham Gazette* that the Avon might be extended to join it by way of Warwick, possibly going on to Coventry. Both this scheme, and the Trent-Severn link discussed above, would have added a Higher Avon to the Upper, and completed Sandys' original plan. Each was stillborn, and the river remained a mere branch off the nation's developing trunk routes.

Relations between the owners of the two halves of the river were not always cordial, and they tended to ignore the opportunity of working together and regarding the whole river as a common enterprise. At the height of these bickerings, George Perrott (the younger) had to seek the help of the Exchequer Court in receiving his share of through tolls taken on the Upper Avon. He should have been paid 4*d.*/ton rather than the 3*d*. which he was given. Trade on the river as a whole was less brisk than it had been in times past: the late 18th century was a time of severe economic depression in the area. In 1769, the slump was so deep that the Stratford Corporation petitioned the Secretary of War against the quartering of two groups of Dragoons there, because 'The weight of the taxes are great and severely felt by the poorer sort of people . . . there is no manufacture established in this place'.

In the following decade, even the traditional Shakespearian Processions stopped because of the decline in prosperity of the local Jersey Combers and Flax Processors who supported them, and in the land tax Survey of 1781 a full tenth of the Houses of Stratford were empty. According to the *Victoria History of the County of Warwick*, the Avon trade declined 'both as a cause and effect' of this depression.

Even during these years of hardship, vessels still found cargoes, and by 1795 the Avon had been so improved by the steady efforts of its owners that the 47 ton barge *Good Intent* regulary traded from Tewkesbury to Stratford. This was

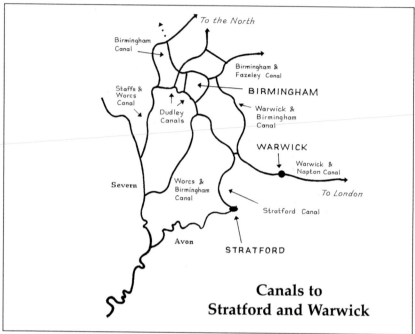

Canals to Stratford and Warwick

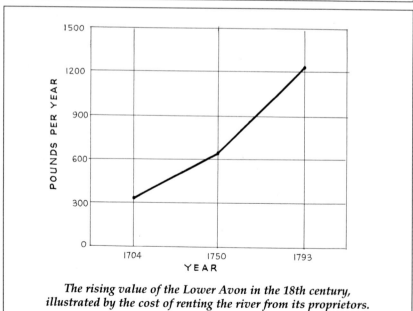

The rising value of the Lower Avon in the 18th century,
illustrated by the cost of renting the river from its proprietors.

about the size of an Upper Severn trow (*see page 78*), and comparable with the broad-beam craft still to be seen on the Leeds and Liverpool Canal. In 1793 George Perrott (the younger) had made enough money to build the magnificent Craycombe House on the banks of the Avon near Fladbury, although some of this wealth would have come from other sources. Dark clouds were gathering on the horizon, however. Times were changing, and Britain's industry, previously strolling at the steady pace of waterwheels and horses' hooves, now marched to the beat of atmospheric steam engines. They may not yet have been powering boats, but they were turning the machinery of factories, and more importantly they were draining the mines growing up in the deep coal measures of South Staffordshire. Birmingham and the Black Country grew quickly in wealth and importance, and in response to its need for efficient transport, more canals were proposed. The year of 1791 saw the passing of an Act with serious consequences for Avon prosperity: 'An Act for making and maintaining a Navigable Canal from or near to the town of Birmingham, in the County of Warwick, to communicate with the river Severn, near the City of Worcester'.

Cheap coal would now travel from the Midlands field, either directly along the new Worcester and Birmingham Canal or along the Staffordshire and Worcestershire Canal, down the Severn, then up the Worcester and Birmingham Canal, to places convenient for land carriage to Evesham and Pershore, in competition with Dean Forest coal coming up the Avon (*see map page 46*). The upper regions of the Severn were to be so improved by the Staffs and Worcs company that navigation would be possible throughout the year, but its lower regions were still difficult to sail. The route for Forest of Dean coal, which came from the south and could be expected to travel along the Avon, would become dangerously uncompetitive.

Resigned to the rise of a new order, Perrott neither opposed the Worcester and Birmingham Act, nor sought compensation from the company, but instead obtained an Act in 1793 (33 Geo.III cap.23) which would allow him to set aside his uncle's will, thus shedding, if he wished, all of his rights in the Lower Avon. The preamble to the Act told the tale clearly:

The said River Avon hath been gradually improved for thirty years past, and is now let on lease, whereof two years or thereabouts are now unexpired, at the rent of £1,227 pa, and could now sell to advantage, but on account of the Navigations that have already taken place, and other Navigations which are still projecting, the Value of such Navigation is become precarious and is attended with a risque which may be dangerous to an individual proprietor.

It can be seen from this that the rent had increased again, from £630 pa to £1,227 pa (a graph of rent versus time is shown in opposite). There were no takers.

During the following decades, the network of inland waterways was to change rapidly. Yarranton's dream of seeing the Avon part of an east-west trunk route was finally killed in 1783, with the passing of an Act for the Thames and Severn Canal. Taking a direct line between the Severn at Framilode and the Thames near Lechlade, this navigation offered a far shorter route than the Severn-Avon-Stour-Cherwell-Thames one envisaged a century previously. Through navigation between London and Birmingham became possible for the first time in 1789. The earliest way, by a few months, was from Birmingham, down the Staffordshire and Worcestershire Canal, via the Severn to Framilode, along the Stroudwater and Thames and Severn Canals, and from Lechlade down the Thames to London. The second, and better, way was along the Birmingham and Fazely to the Coventry Canal, thence down the Oxford Canal and so to the Thames at Oxford. The effects on the old routes of land carriage were dramatic:

> . . . since the canal from Birmingham to Coventry had been compleated the Land Carriage from Bristol and Worcester through Stratford and Warwick to Coventry has decreased three fourths.

Warwick grain markets had been traditionally supplied from the North Warwickshire and Oxfordshire by road. Now, this movement of goods

> . . . has however greatly decreased since the junction of the Birmingham and Fazely Canal with the Coventry and the Markets at Warwick have visibly declined . . . to recover this lost traffic (with increase) is a principal object of the Inhabitants [of Warwick] by obtaining a Canal, which scheme they say they have been almost compell'd to adopt from the Conduct of their neighbour at Stratford who had previously adopted a similar project for some time carried on by them with much secrecy . . .

By August 1792 the merchant Peter Holford chaired a committee to promote a canal from Stratford with a branch to Warwick, linking to either the Digbeth branch of the Birmingham Canal, or to the Worcester and Birmingham. Meanwhile, the proprietors of the Dudley Canal (which connected the Staffordshire and Worcester line, via the Stourbridge, through Dudley to the Birmingham Canal) had decided to extend their cut through a new tunnel at Lapal to join the Worcester and Birmingham Canal at Selly Oak. This 'Dudley No. 2' line formed a route for traffic bound south from the Black Country which by-passed the tolls of the Birmingham Canal. This was to influence the Stratford Committee who could benefit from the through route, and they decided to join their canal to the Worcester and Birmingham at King's Norton (*see map page 48*).

The Birmingham Canal Company was unhappy with the prospect of losing its south-bound business to the Dudley No. 2 Canal, and brought pressure to bear on those who wished to connect with it. Under this stress, the Warwick and Stratford Committees split, the former building the narrow Warwick and Birmingham Canal, now part of the broad Grand Union Canal main line to London. (It is interesting to note that, four centuries after Richard de Beauchamp had first seen the advantages of bringing a navigable river to the county town, the new Earl of Warwick was foremost amongst those building the canal.)

The Stratford group obtanied an Act for a quite separate Stratford Canal, to King's Norton, passed on 28th March, 1793. Interestingly, there was no provision for joining the canal to the River Avon, presumably because the prospect of a through route from the lower Severn to Birmingham would have worried the Worcester and Birmingham Canal Company, who would then not have agreed to the King's Norton Junction. The common story of lack of funding made the building of the canal a slow and difficult process, and not until 1816 did the first boat pass through it into Stratford-upon-Avon.

The prospect of a canal in Stratford unconnected with the River posed a very serious problem to the proprietors of the Avon Navigations! Coal from the Midlands could travel far more easily than that from the Severn, and the same went for other produce. In 1814, even before the canal had actually reached Stratford, a guide book tells of the decline in the Avon trade. Until a few years ago, the River Avon had been

> . . . of immense advantage to the town and neighbouring country, in conveying all sorts of merchandise from Bristol, Gloucester, Tewkesbury, Worcester etc., into the inland part of the Kingdom, the barges returning with the natural and artificial produce of the country. Statford had then the appearance of a small sea-port town; at present however, in consequence of the numerous canals, and the unparalleled improvement in turnpike roads, the trade by water is considerably diminished.

Two people took a special interest in joining the canal to the Avon in an attempt to generate river-borne traffic in the down direction. One of these was, not surprisingly, George Perrott who stood to loose more than anybody. His partner in the campaign, William James, was an ambitious engineer whose determination was largely responsible for the completion of the Stratford Canal itself. Destined to play a significant rôle in the development of Stratford-upon-Avon, with other works which dominate a later chapter in this book, James bought all of the shares in the Upper Avon in 1813, ⅖ leasehold and ⅗ freehold. In 1815, he managed to get a new Act passed, authorising a junction with the river.

On the canal's opening day, in a passenger boat they had borrowed from the Worcester and Birmingham company, the Stratford Canal Committee travelled from Wootton Wawen to Stratford. They were followed by 20 narrow-boats laden with coal. R.B. Wheler reported: 'This covered boat, crowded to excess, was the first which entered the Avon, amidst the rejoicings of many thousand people . . . I was at the very head of this boat, that thus wedded the Avon'.

The proprietors of the river had thus won a partial victory, because although they had lost much of the upstream coal trade, they had gained one in the other direction. This was in fact the trading pattern which Sandys had envisaged nearly two centuries before! From its point of view, the Worcester and Birmingham Canal Company need not have worried. Its route from Birmingham to the Severn at Worcester and thence to the end of the Avon at Tewkesbury was 40½ miles, containing 59 locks, as against 67¾ miles and 72 locks via the Stratford Canal and the Avon. In addition, the persistent lack of a horse towing path made the Avon an even slower route.

It may seem rather odd, on the face of it, that in the time of the 'canal mania', when vast capital was mobilised to build fairly expensive canals, little was done in the way of improvement to river navigations. While it is true that water transport by canal is a little more efficient that by river (a single horse could pull a maximum of 50 tons as opposed to 30 - on the best roads the maximum was 2 tons), rivers still had potential advantages. Compared to the building of a brand new canal, with costs of land acquisition as well as immense construction works, the improvement of rivers was relatively cheap. Also, because the limiting dimensions of river craft are usually determined by lock sizes rather than channel sizes, making a river waterway for large barges is far more feasible. Rivers meander, it is true, but then so did the early canals - Brindley's Oxford line has a section which curves for 11 miles to link towns four miles apart! Risks from flood damage were a very real problem with rivers, as the 1758 destruction of the Calder and Hebble Navigation witnessed, but then ice in the winters (far colder then, at the tail end of the 'little ice age') and drought in the summer were serious handicaps to canals. To see why rivers were so starved of resources whilst speculators queued to support artificial cuts one must look beyond rational comparisons, to examine the prejudices of the time.

Brindley, usually (but somewhat incorrectly, in view of earlier achievements) called 'the Father of British canals', held navigable rivers in contempt. It is widely recounted that, when asked by a Member of Parliament what use rivers were in the canal age, he replied that there best use was to supply canals with water! Perhaps this bias against rivers stemmed from his fear of their destructive floods, but it may as well have originated in the long legal fight he had with the proprietors of the Irwell Navigation when he built the Bridgewater Canal to Manchester. Whatever the causes, the fact was that while new canals were opened, sometimes at a rate of more than one per year, the ancient rivers which linked the canal network to the sea never saw neither speculators nor their money. Ironically, the poor state of the rivers at their termini was to be the death of some canals: the Thames and Severn, joining the practically unnavigable upper Thames at Lechlade, is a prime example. An even greater irony has developed in recent years, when the small dimensions of Brindley's cuts has made them too unprofitable to carry goods, but rivers have been improved for huge barges and coasters. Now the map of freight-carrying waterways looks almost as it did before Brindley was born.

Given that public finance for improvement was unlikely to be forthcoming, George Perrott had handled the builders of the canals with impressive skill. When the Stratford Company was negotiating about whether they would make the junction with the Worcester and Birmingham at King's Norton, or the Birmingham Canal at Digbeth, he gave his support to the group which favoured the King's Norton branch, also the favourite of the Worcester and Birmingham who owned it, *on condition that* the Stratford Committee would get in their Bill a clause in his favour. This was to stipulate that if he should suffer enough losses due to the Worcester and Birmingham to reduce his receipts below their current figure of £1227 pa, the latter company should make them up to that figure. Once the Stratford Canal was completed, the payments would fall to £400 pa, the level which stands today. Thus protected from the loss of income, Perrott joined the canal mania, owning 35 shares in 1803 and 30 when he died on 5th January, 1806.

On the death of George Perrott, the rights in the river passed to his son George Wigley Perrott. With this succession there started a decline in the fortune of the family, displayed by a series of mortgages, the first of which was for two-thirds of the Avon shares for £2,000, in October 1812. The income from the river cannot be blamed for this, because it was not until 1813 that the receipts first fell below £1,227 pa and even then the deficiency was of course paid by the Worcester and Birmingham Company.

The growing traffic coming from canals brought a new type of boat to the Avon. Brindley's first canal, the Bridgewater, was deep and broad, and able to be used by traditional river craft (Mersey Flats, 70 ft long and 14 ft broad). In order to economise in the building of his subsequent canals, which required expensive tunnels and cuttings and were less well endowed with water, he decided to reduce the maximum beam of vessels by approximately half. The resulting 'narrow-boats',* were 70 feet long and just under seven feet wide, and became the dominant craft of the Midlands canal system. At first, such oddly-shaped craft were considered unsuitable for use on river navigations, and their cargoes were transhipped to conventional trows at basins such as those at Stourport-on-Severn, Diglis (Worcester) and Stratford. Gradually it was realised that there was no reason that narrow-boats should not be used on rivers in normal conditions, and they began to appear on the Severn as far south as Gloucester. Their increasing presence off the canals soon revealed an unexpected barrier to trade as far as the Lower Avon was concerned; one of its locks was too short to admit a 70 ft hull. On being informed of the problem by the Worcester and Birmingham Committee, Perrott promised to deal with the matter, and to offer 'every facility to boats etc. carried on the Avon from Tewkesbury'.

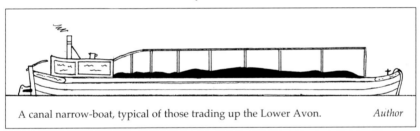

A canal narrow-boat, typical of those trading up the Lower Avon.   *Author*

The difficulties facing navigators of Upper River were much greater. The minute book of the Proprietors of the Stratford Canal stated that they were hampered by the 'delipidated state of the locks on the Avon Navigation preventing Boats going down to Evesham'. William James, who owned the Upper River, closed it for repairs during the summer and early autumn of 1822 and spent £6,000 on heavy refurbishment of the works. However, the remains of the locks of the Upper river are, in some cases, shorter than 70 feet, so would still not have admitted full length narrow-boats from the canal; transshipment at Stratford would be required. The extra expense of transhipment, coupled with a reduction in Worcester and Birmingham tolls, combined to discourage traffic from using the Upper Avon at all.

The fortunes of its owner, who will play a leading rôle in a subsequent chapter, declined. By 1823, he could not repay a loan because of losses made on the inefficient river. He tried to sell up, and said that he was hopeful that G.W. Perrott would buy it, the river having potential for the new steam-boats that were beginning to appear over 100 years after Hulls' experiment. His optimism was unfounded, and at the Royal Hotel Birmingham in June 1824, the river was

---

* Vessels of the narrow-boat type were also known as long-boats on the Severn and Avon systems. Authorities differ on the need for a hyphen in both terms.

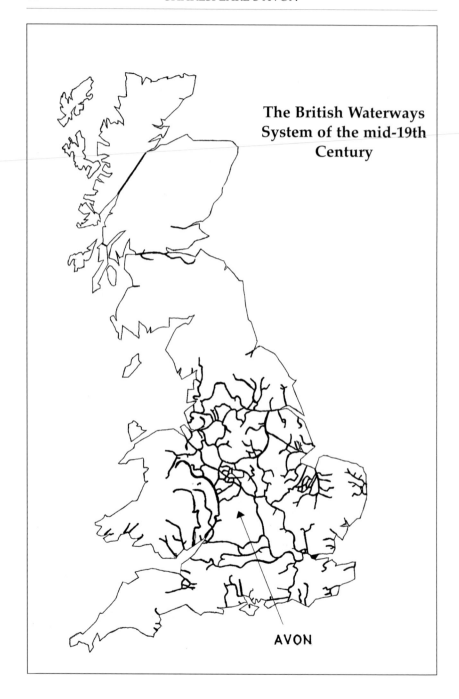

The British Waterways
System of the mid-19th
Century

AVON

auctioned together with other assets of the now bankrupt William James. It was purchased for £5,000 by a syndicate of the following people:

Richard Gresley	Robert Atty	Timothy Smith
John Greaves	John Welchman Whately	Abel Peynton
Rev. John Ellis (Vicar of Wooton Wawen)		

The syndicate (referred to as the Avon Navigation Co. in the *Victoria History of Warwickshire*) carried out further improvements to the Navigation. As well as following the traditional pattern of dredging and scouring, they created a brand new staircase lock (a double-lock, the top gates of one chamber serving as the bottom ones for the next) at Lucy's Mill, Stratford. This mill, one of the largest on the river, became an increasingly important customer for river-borne grain, which was processed into flour for sale in the local area, and also taken up the Stratford Canal to the rapidly expanding market of Midlands industrial towns. An indirect bonus to the trade of the river was realised in 1827, when the Gloucester and Sharpness Ship Canal was at last completed. The Severn, tidal up to Worcester in those times, had always been a difficult river to navigate in its lowest reaches, and the sandbanks between Gloucester and Lydney created such an obstruction that barges could pass over them on only a few days each month, around spring tides. On neap tides, cargo-laden Trows would have to waste valuable days tied up at Gloucester's Roman Quay, or at anchor in King Road (Avonmouth), just waiting. The immense new canal provided a by-pass, complete with tow path, and allowed ships to travel between Gloucester and the Bristol Channel every day.

In the year before George Wigley Perrott died, an agreement between the syndicate and Perrott abandoned the double toll system at Evesham, Upper Avon tolls being valid to half a mile below Evesham bridge and Lower Avon tolls being valid to half a mile above it. Perrott fought hard to stop this at first, and the syndicate of the Upper Avon had to go to the King's Bench to achieve it. The river was clearly able to carry a trade in spite of competition. For the next 40 years the boats continued to ply its waters, and the river basked in a kind of Indian Summer before its eventual fall.

Craycombe Manor, built by George Perrot (the younger).   *Author*

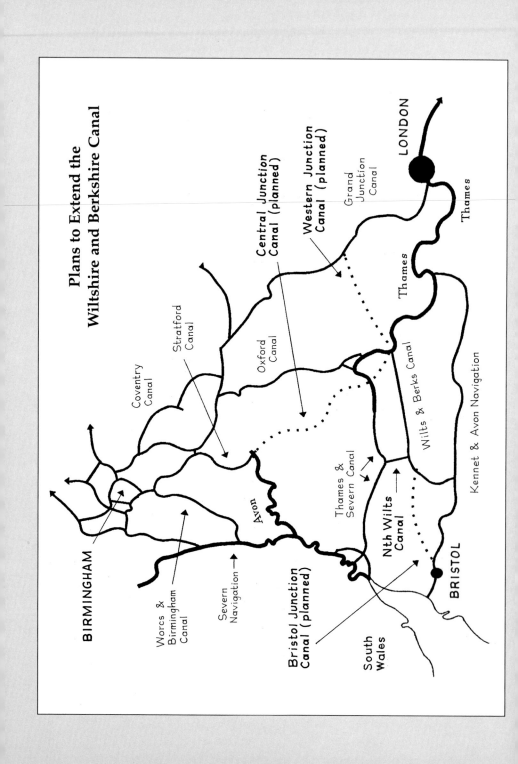

Plans to Extend the
Wiltshire and Berkshire Canal

Chapter Seven

More Great Plans

Nearly a century and a half after Yarranton had published his book, plans were made once again to place Stratford at the centre of a far-reaching transport network linking the Thames, the Severn, and the Midlands. Two schemes were suggested, the first having its roots planted firmly in the canal age, and the second looking ahead, with a vision akin to those of Andrew Yarranton and Jonathan Hulls, to the fiery iron horses of times to come.

One of the least important navigations to be built in Southern England, forgotten by all but the small band of enthusiasts currently setting about its restoration, was the Wiltshire and Berkshire Canal. The main line of this narrow, largely agricultural waterway ran from Semington on the Kennet and Avon line, to Abingdon on the Thames, and served the local communities of Wiltshire and the White Horse Vale (*see map opposite*). In 1810, more than a decade after the 'canal mania' had finished, its owners considered proposals for four new branches, designed to develop their sleepy rural concern into a major trunk route. One, the North Wilts branch, was to connect with the broad Thames and Severn Canal at Latton, near Cricklade, and allow narrow-boats to by-pass the shallow Upper Thames completely. Another, the Western Junction, was to connect Abingdon with the Grand Junction Canal, allowing traffic between the Severn basin and London to avoid the Thames entirely. The Bristol Junction was to play a similar rôle in allowing this traffic to by-pass the Somerset Avon. From the point of view of Shakespeare's Avon, the most important proposal was also the most ambitious - the 'Central Junction Canal'. A map, which can still be found in Warwickshire Record Office, records its projected route - from Abingdon, via Fyfield, Bampton, Great Rissington, Bourton-on-the-Water, Bourton-on-the-Hill and Shipston-on-Stour, to Stratford-upon-Avon.

The effect this canal may have had on local trading patterns cannot be predicted exactly, of course, but the following assumptions may be made with some degree of confidence. Locally, the tradesmen of Stratford would have gained a waterway through the heartlands of Cotswolds agriculture and quarrying, thereby regaining much of the ancient trade lost to the Oxford and the Warwick and Napton canals. By the same token, Midlands coal and industrial produce would enjoy an easy route to this area via the Stratford Canal. Depending on how heavily locked it had turned out to be, the waterway may also have offered a useful alternative to the Warwick and Birmingham, Warwick and Napton, and Oxford Canal route for boats plying between Birmingham and the Upper Thames. The tradesmen of Stratford-upon-Avon could therefore look forward to benefit a good deal from the opening of the Central Junction.

What of the Avon? The proposed line from Stratford met the Wilts and Berks Canal at its eastern end, so would not interfere with river-borne traffic between Stratford and the Bristol Channel. However, its northern parts, by serving the

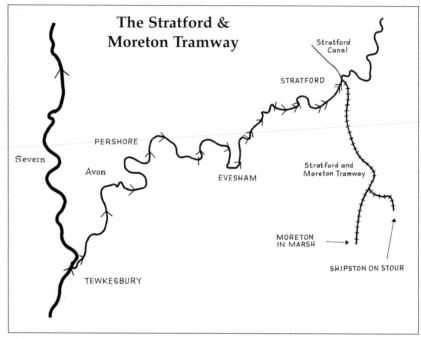

The sole survivor of the Stratford and Moreton Tramway's rolling stock, this crude wagon now stands on a short length of track, next to the Bancroft canal basin.

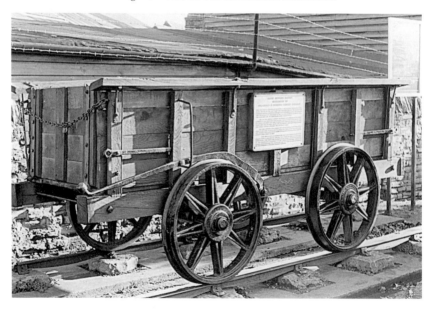

Cotswolds, would have had both deleterious and beneficial effects on Upper Avon Tolls. In the absence of a canal, Cotswold towns such as Moreton-in-Marsh exported and imported goods by road as far as Evesham, and thence by water either downstream to the Severn, or upstream to Stratford and the canal system. Were the proposed Central Junction Canal to be built, the Upper Avon would lose its carriage of Cotswolds to Midlands goods completely. Offsetting this loss would have been the route from the Cotswolds, via the new canal, towards the Severn Basin.

The area through which the canal was to run is famed for the beauty of its hilly country, and the Central Junction would have been very difficult and expensive to build. For this reason, it gained only weak support from its friends, and suffered strong opposition from other canal companies with whom it would compete. Like Yarranton's proposed Avon/Severn link, the idea faded away into the near oblivion of a County Record Office's dusty shelves.

The second scheme was the brainchild of the same William James who came to own the Upper Avon. His father, also called William, had become heavily involved in the canal mania, and like so many other investors, had suffered heavy losses through unwise speculation. The younger William fared much better with his own interests. By the time he was 40, he was the wealthy owner of several large collieries (Wyken near Coventry, Swadlincote, and West Bromwich), and was worth an estimated £150,000. Following in his father's footsteps, he bought a substantial number of shares in the Stratford Canal Company, and served on its committee between 1805 and 1821, rising to the post of Chairman; were it not for his enthusiasm, the line would probably never have been completed.

Possibly inspired by the stillborn plans for the Central Junction Canal, to which he would have been privy, William James became interested in the creation of a Central Junction Railway. At this time, railways had not yet reached their infancy, and were limited to very small lines serving coal and iron fields in Northumbria, the South Wales valleys, and Surrey. Locomotives were just beginning to make a hesitant appearance - most notably Trevithick's pioneering steam engine which ran a Welsh canal-feeding tramroad. The glorious expresses and the great trunk routes of Stephenson and Brunel lay far in the future. Seen in the context of his time, the scheme of William James was remarkable indeed. He envisaged that a railway should be built from Stratford, by way of Shipston, Moreton-in-Marsh, Oxford, Thame, and Uxbridge, to the City of London itself, with a branch from Shipston to his own Wyken Colliery. Using the canal to carry goods further north, his line would have provided a new trunk route from London to the industrial heartlands, with economic effects similar to that of the earlier canal scheme, but with the potential for much more. Though it was yet to prove itself, James had realised that steam traction was to be the future of transport, and intended from the beginning that locomotives be used on his railway.

A visionary, only just too far ahead of his time, the author of this ambitions scheme was unable to raise financial support for the building of his railway in its entirety. He did, however, gain sufficient backing from his friend Lord Redesdale, who lived near Moreton-in-Marsh, to construct the part of the

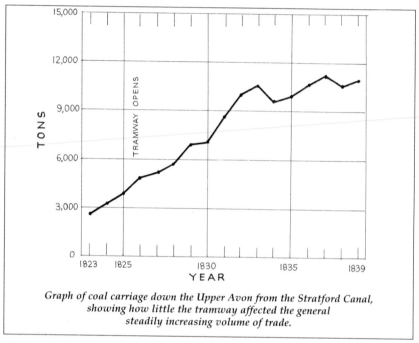

*Graph of coal carriage down the Upper Avon from the Stratford Canal,
showing how little the tramway affected the general
steadily increasing volume of trade.*

The Stratford and Moreton's brick viaduct over the Avon. Though the tramway is
unlikely to be restored, much of its route has become a footpath, and may still be enjoyed
by those with the time to explore and to listen for echoes of William James' dreams.

Author

railway running from there to Stratford, as a feeder to the canal. A public meeting was held in Moreton on 14th August, 1820, and Royal Assent to the Bill for a 16-mile tramway was obtained on 28th May, 1821. Members of Parliament were beginning to become familiar with this type of Bill, having passed a similar one six weeks earlier. The latter enabled the supporters of the Stockton and Darlington Canal to build a railway in place of their planned navigation, appointing as Engineer a certain George Stephenson. The railway age had begun.

During the building of the Stratford and Moreton Railway, James maintained his interest in steam traction, and travelled north to view some of Stephenson's colliery locomotives. He reported back very favourably, and told the company that the best locomotive choice for its line, the *Invention*, could be delivered complete to Stratford for £440. Faced with this high price, and with their concern over the costs of maintaining track suitable for heavy machinery, the committee split over the question of steam versus horses. Unable to decide between the enthusiasm of William James, and the natural caution of more conservative shareholders, they canvassed the opinion of independent engineers. Unhelpfully, these too were divided; Thomas Telford advised against steam while John Rastrick opined that, while current locomotives may not be powerful enough for the Cotswold banks, the railway could make good use of future developments, and should be built with steam in mind.

As construction proceeded, the story of the Stratford Canal repeated itself, and money ran out. Faced with escalating costs, the railway company had to request a new Bill from Parliament, authorising it to raise more money. It won, but at terrible cost: with the company at their mercy, a few landowners insisted in the insertion of a clause forbidding the use of steam traction between Aldington and Stratford, where the railway followed the road. Without through running, the advantages of locomotive power could not be realised, and William James' ambitious ideas were stopped in their tracks. Though his planned Central Junction Railway had suffered a mortal wound, he refused to accept defeat, and even surveyed an extension from Moreton to Shipton-under-Wychwood. It was never built.*

In 1826, the main line of the horse-drawn Stratford and Moreton railway was completed, the Shipston branch following a decade later. Though celebrated locally, the opening met with little national attention. A full year previously, Stephenson's Stockton and Darlington Railway opened; its trains, drawn by smoke-belching horses of iron, set a model for the world.

Obsolescent even when new, the Stratford and Moreton Tramway nevertheless carried a considerable tonnage of freight, and even sported a passenger sevice. Though problems with interest payments and with repairs to poorly-constructed permanent way prevented a profit being made in the early years, from about 1830 the company received a good return from its little line. The antiquated tramway survived until early this century, still being worked according to the rules laid down in its intitial Act of Incorporation. Born of the canal age, its operation was more similar to that of a waterway or turnpike than to later railway lines. While the company owned and maintained the permanent way, traders were free to use their own 'trains' as and when they

---

* The tramway surveyed by William James was followed, more or less, by the Oxford, Worcester and Wolverhampton Railway many years later, in its line from Oxford to Moreton.

pleased (with special rules governing passing priorities on the single track). For safety, all waggons had to conform to specifications of weight (4 tons), gauge and braking. One solitary example is preserved on a short length of original plateway in Stratford-upon-Avon's Bancroft Gardens (*see page 58*). It is probably quite typical, though according to one account some vehicles were provided with a platform on which the horse could ride, when the 'train' was descending a gradient, hopefully under the control of its prominent handbrake.

Although it provided an easy route between the Cotswolds and the Midlands, bypassing the Upper Avon, the tramway had little effect on the tonnages carried by the river (*see graph on page 60*). Indeed it had little effect on anything; the towns of Stratford, Moreton and Shipston continued much as before, with none of the tremendous growth associated with the 'railway towns' of Stephenson and Brunel. The revolutions of the mid-19th century passed them by, and the economies of the North Cotswolds and the Avon valley remained faithful to the patterns of five decades before. Yet again, a great dream had faded away. The face of George Stephenson appears on every five pound note, but that of William James is all but forgotten.

Offenham weir, with the Upper Avon syndicate's new lock to the right.   *Charles Showell*

Chapter Eight

1827 to 1860:
Swan Song of a River

During the 18th and early 19th centuries, the design of steam engines improved dramatically, first with James Watt's idea of condensing steam in a container separate from the main cylinder, resulting in a massive increase in efficiency, and then with development of small, high-pressure engines. The great improvement in power-to-weight ratio allowed by both of these developments vastly expanded the application of the machines and made marine propulsion a practical proposition. Twenty years after James Watt's 1763 patent, Jacques Perrier's little experimental craft made its first historic journey against the current of the Seine, and by 1802 Scotland saw the first successful British steamer, the famous *Charlotte Dundas*; the age of the powered boat had arrived.

The use of steam to power vessels, which was faster and cheaper than the traditional practice of bow-hauling, made trade on the Avon a more economical proposition than it had been. Paddle steamers began to appear on the Severn from 1814, when a fast passenger boat plied between Worcester and Gloucester in 4½ hours - an impressive average speed of over 6 knots. In 1830,* the idea of using a steam vessel to tug unpowered barges was introduced, by Humphrey Brown and Son of Tewkesbury. Their boat, *Sabrina*, possessed two 14 hp engines, mounted horizontally to minimize air draught (height above water). Two years later, this boat gained an all too literal victory over her sailing rivals, by colliding with the ninety-ton Trow, *Neptune*, and sinking her! After steam had proved successful on the Severn, it was introduced on its tributary. In 1827, soon after the opening of the Gloucester and Sharpness Canal, the minute book of the proprietors of the Stratford Canal recorded that:

A steam vessel has been worked on the river from Bristol to Stratford Mills, and some spirited individuals are about forming a company for the establishment of a regular communication between Stratford and Bristol.

The boat was owned by Thomas Lucy and Son of Stratford Mills, and it was bought to supply 3,000 bushels (24,000 gallons) per week of Irish corn. The navigation works were steadily improved by the syndicate for the Upper Avon, to enable barges of deeper draught, and consequently greater burden, to navigate up to Stratford. Troublesome shoals, which had limited the loads which could be carried in the dry months, were dredged away, and then effort was expended in modernisation of the locks. In Sandys' time, the shallowness of the reaches downstream of Luddington, Welford and Harvington weirs had been a major handicap to the navigation. Yarranton and his contemporaries had built water-gates below each of these shallows, and had thus achieved some improvement. However, use of the water-gates was extremely slow, and their weirs were still too low for 19th century vessels. The Upper Avon Syndicate therefore rebuilt

* Cox refers to a steam boat service between Evesham and Newport, South Wales, running from 1763 to 1788. In view of the known facts about steam engineering, this is extremely unlikely. Perhaps the author meant 1863-1888?

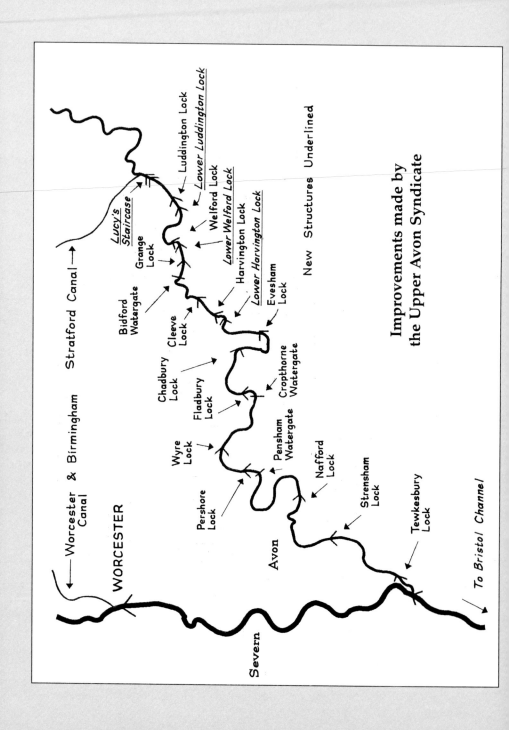

Improvements made by
the Upper Avon Syndicate

them as proper pound locks with higher weirs. The chambers of Lower Luddington, Lower Welford, and Lower Harvington (Offenham) locks were rectangular, following normal canal practice, in clear contrast to the circle and diamond built by the earlier engineers. The work was completed in 1828, and left Bidford the only water-gate above Evesham. The rebuilt navigation was described as being suitable throughout the year, for barges of up to 30 tons capacity. In June 1832, the Chairman of the Stratford Canal Company said that 'every shilling of the tonnage of every description received by the Avon Company had been expended in the improvement of the Navigation'.

In that year, the Upper Avon Syndicate bought land by the canal basin at Stratford and built their own warehouse there, and in the next year bought the Upper and Lower Ham to use as wharfs. *West's Directory of Warwickshire* enthused '. . . the Navigation of the beautiful River Avon is now under the management of its spirited and respectable proprietors, becoming all that can be expected, for the purposes of trade, on a river'.

The improvements did indeed cause an increase in trade. Lucy's steamer was travelling the round trip from Stratford to Gloucester in three days, while two Bristol companies were sending weekly barges up the river loaded with Bristol and Gloucester goods. One of the Bristol companies even built its own wharf at Evesham.

The success of the Stratford Canal caused an increase in Midland coal traffic downstream towards Evesham, as illustrated by their proprietors' minute book. In 1823, 1825 and 1832 the tonnages were 2,598, 3,804 and 9,997 tons respectively. The large increase between the figures for 1825 and 1832 was due in part to a strategic manipulation of tolls: vessels travelling down to the lower reaches of the Avon from the Stratford Canal, thus competing with those supplied from the Worcester and Birmingham, were encouraged by a 'drawback' which reduced their net tolls.

In this same competitive spirit, the Worcester and Birmingham Company sent a deputation to George Wigley Perrott, 'with power to treat with him for taking the tolls of the Lower Navigation of the River Avon'. By taking control of the lower Avon, the Worcester & Birmingham would have an effective monopoly on Severn-Midlands traffic unless it travelled by the Staffs and Worcs Canal, and would also take tolls on any freight from the Stratford Canal which ventured beyond Evesham. Perrott replied that Thomas Milton wanted the river for one more year, after which he was ready to negotiate. In 1830, wishing to obtain several offers for his river, thereby to increase its price, Perrott advertised it in *Berrow's Worcester Journal*, informing prospective customers that:

> The Trade in Coal, as well as in Grain, Flour, Timber and Merchandise of all descriptions is very considerable and capable of improvement by any spirited individual or individuals willing to give attention to its capabilities.

Whether he got any replies from outside the canal company is not recorded, but their battle against rival canals gave them a special reason for wanting it, even at a high price. In July of that year, the Worcester and Birmingham leased the Lower Avon for 21 years at £1,000 pa, less £120 pa for undertaking to maintain the river and replace 11 lock gates with ones of equivalent quality to those installed by

Perrott. They renewed their lease, in 1851, for another 21 years. The lease allowed the Worcester and Birmingham Canal to profit both from the Midlands coal travelling down to the Severn, and also from rival Forest of Dean coal travelling up from it. In addition, it prevented the Stratford Canal Company from selling its coal further downstream than Evesham, without paying a toll to its rival. Keen to maintain competition, the Worcester & Birmingham set its rates low, and in June 1833 the Stratford Canal Proprietors' minute book said that if their own tolls were not reduced 'coals by the Worcester and Birmingham Canal and up the Avon, would be brought cheaper to Evesham and would put a total stop to any coal going down the Avon from Stratford'. Striking back, the Stratford Canal Company granted a further reduction of 8d./ton on coal carried down to Pershore, by the carrier J.B. Baugh.

The Perrott fortunes continued their decline, and in 1835 his estate went into receivership with a total debt in excess of £13,000. The receiver, one E.W. Oldaker, happened to be a shareholder in the Stratford Canal. The circumstances surrounding the bankruptcy and its outcome are confused, but what seems to have happened is that a Perrott Trust retained at least partial ownership of the river, while the operating rights were sold off to a Lower Avon Navigation Company. Certainly the family name continued to arise in connection with the Lower Avon until the Perrott Trust sold it about a century later. The financial failure of G.W. Perrott could not, in all fairness, be laid at the door of his navigation. At this time, it still sported a fairly regular traffic, helped perhaps by the fact that three new locks on the Severn made great improvements to that river's traffic in the 1840s. *Bentley's Directory* of 1840 lists two carriers, Joseph Judd and William Wilks, each operating a weekly barge service up and downstream from Evesham, Wilks originally being an agent to the Bristol company, Barnetts, who also operated barges on the river. Two years later, Judd and Wilks amalgamated, offering an additional service along the Stratford and Moreton Tramway. As well as carrying cargoes, the trading companies also offered warehousing facilities and quays and wharfs for trading - much of Evesham's riverside, today bare green parkland, was covered by these buildings.

Since the upper river had been owned by its flamboyant engineer, William James, the Stratford Canal Company had been connected in some loose way with the Avon Navigation. Their connection was to be strengthened when the proprietors of the Upper Avon, 6/7 of whom were shareholders in the canal, offered the lease of their river to the canal company, allowing the latter to meet Worcester and Birmingham territory head on at Evesham. Beginning on 1st July, 1842, the lease ran for five years, costing the canal £400 for the first year, and £450 per annum subsequently. This, the first formal association between canal and upper river, was to be the beginning of the latter's ruin.

Even after so much money had been spent by William James and by the Upper Avon Syndicate, the state of the river compared poorly with that of nearby navigations, especially the canals. In his delightful guidebook, *Rambles by Rivers - The Avon*, James Thorne described the scene at Luddington in 1845: 'a primitive looking, clumsy lock, a rude wooden hut, and a foaming weir'.

Observing the slow passage of a barge, he concluded that the operation of the navigation was,

. . . conducted in a primitive fashion. Horses were not employed to draw barges at first, nor are they now. At a huge heavy-laden craft five or six strong men may be seen tugging laboriously . . . It is said that a horse-path could not be made along the riverside without an expensive process . . . It is a painful sight to see these men dragging their barge along this river, which from its many curves would be extremely hard work for horses.

Under these conditions, with competition coming from improved roads and a by now comprehensive canal network, trade on the Upper Avon could longer balance the expense of its maintenance. The Stratford Canal Company lost £68 in 1842, and £89 in both 1843 and 1844; anxious not to throw good money after bad, its committee relinquished its lease on 30th June, 1847. The Upper Avon's Syndicate were now in an uncomfortable position. Their river, with its trade badly affected by canals and turnpike roads and to a small extent by the tramway, could no longer pay its way. In past times of trouble, there had been the hope that circumstances may one day improve and that the local economy would once again make the Avon financially viable. This time, however, none but the most indefatigable optimist could entertain such a feeling. Waterways were being made obsolete by the wealth they had created - that the canal-building mania had ceased was no comfort to those watching the 'railway mania' arrive.

The first of the new iron roads to take river-borne trade was the Oxford, Worcester and Wolverhampton Railway (OW&WR) (*see map page 68*), which was running trains from Kidderminster to Evesham by 1852. By offering yet another route from the Midlands to the Vale of Evesham, and one which omitted Stratford and the Upper Avon altogether, the railway bit deeply into the operating profits of coal barges. River traders, such as Rice and Co. who operated a daily boat service up and down the river, assumed that the canal company wished to fight back and appealed for a reduction of tolls.

Unfortunately, the Avon was trapped by a conflict of interest; even though the lease to the Stratford Canal Company had ceased, the fact that most of the Upper Avon's owners had a large financial stake in that canal meant that the latter was still in effective control. Sadly, the canal company's shareholders were in no mood to fight an upstart railway. They realised that they were unlikely to triumph in the long run, and that their best hope of getting a return on investment was to sell out to the competition while they could still command a good price. The OW&WR had already bought the Stourbridge Extension canal in similar circumstances, and was rumoured to be interested in any other waterways in its territory. Consequently, the Stratford shareholders had no wish to antagonize them, and the requested reduction in river tolls was not forthcoming. Traffic fell to a mere trickle.

During the 1850s, the Upper Avon's owners tried to sell their almost moribund river for as little as £150, but nobody would buy it. By 1857, they simply gave up and ceased to take tolls, leaving the river in the hands of its few remaining carriers, and the elements which threatened its navigation works.

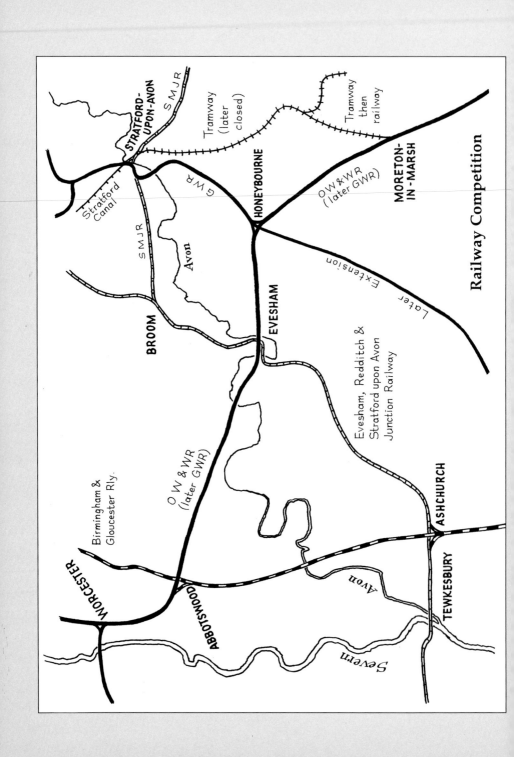

Railway Competition

Chapter Nine

Railroaded

The few boatmen who still plied the Upper Avon had to battle their way along a navigation which was becoming progressively more difficult to work as its locks fell into disrepair and water levels fell. Faced with this unhappy situation, they wished it to be looked after by another navigation company as soon as possible. By the time that the Upper Avon Syndicate had stopped taking tolls, the Stratford Canal had been purchased, as planned, by the OW&WR, who employed a Mr John Broughton to manage it on their behalf. In buying the canal, the railway company had shown themselves to be interested in running navigations where these would provide them with extra 'territory' - rival railway companies had a competition ethic even stronger than that of the waterway rivals of years gone by. Perhaps the OW&WR could be persuaded to purchase the Avon as a logical extension to its canal? With this possibility in mind, the river carriers approached Broughton who, after consultation with Sherriff, the General Manager of the OW&WR, agreed to the purchase for a single payment of £300.

Exactly what passed between these two men as they discussed the Upper Avon's future has never been elucidated - a few years later the contents of the conversation, were they known, would have been crucially important in determining whether the navigation should live or die. One of the decisions which the men are *known* to have reached was that maintenance of the Upper River was to be supported by the receipts of the canal. The agreement, dated 1st March, 1859 and made by Whately, a surviving member of the 1825 syndicate who still technically owned the river, gave Broughton outright possession of $\frac{7}{15}$ of the Upper Avon and a lease on the other $\frac{9}{15}$. Broughton was to receive:

. . . the liberty, privilage, right, benefit and advantage of Navigation and passage for Boats, Trows, Barges, Lighters, Rafts and other vessels . . . from the town of Evesham . . . into the town of Stratford-upon-Avon . . . and also all the estate, right and interest which may belong to the Vendors of and in all locks, weirs and sluices.

Significantly for later events, Broughton himself (and not the OW&WR) was named as the buyer. However, a Board meeting entry of 27th January, 1859 has the OW&WR recording that a Mr Sherriff was officially sent details, by Broughton, of the offer of £300; this would not have been necessary if it was a purely private arrangement. Adding important weight to the conclusion that the railway, and not its manager, owned the waterway, a Board meeting of the GWR quoted in *The Railway Times*, 10th March, 1877 recorded that the Upper Avon 'had been acquired in the interests of the Oxford, Worcester and Wolverhampton in 1860, as a feeder to the Stratford canal'.

Along with the OW&WR, the river passed to the West Midland Railway in 1860, and in 1863 this concern became part of the empire of the mighty Great Western Railway.

The presence of the new iron roads proved insufficient to drive all traffic from the Avon, and the GWR took river toll receipts of between £43 and £151 pa in those years - far from a fortune, but better than nothing. The persistence of water-borne traffic in the face of railway development often surprises people brought up on the school-book version of industrial history. The sheer speed of railways in the age of steam is frequently assumed to have made slow water transport uneconomical almost overnight. In fact, nothing could be further from the truth. Boats may have travelled at only 3 mph but they did this all day, and travelled under the control of only two or three people from source to destination. Railway wagons may have travelled at over ten times the speed of boats, but they were prone to spending much of their time in sidings and yards not moving at all. The higher levels of manning on railways also worked against their use where a good waterway alternative existed. In practice, water transport of non-perishable goods between waterside industries or docks persisted throughout Britain, surrendering finally not to the train but to the lorry. With much Avon traffic moving between Avonmouth docks and riverside mills, there was still an excellent economic justification for river-borne goods.

Even while it enjoyed this small remaining traffic, the state of the railway-owned Navigation worsened. Giving evidence in 1863 for the Redditch and Evesham Railway, a farmer of Salford Priors said of the Upper River: 'The disadvantage . . . is now very much greater since the Great Western had it than before - formerly the locks were kept up in good condition up to Stratford whereas the West Midland [the railway company that bought the OW&WR] have bought it and no one attends the locks'.

A decade later, Welford New Lock was described as being 'useless and broken, part of it being swept away the remainder hanging on, disconsolate and weary'.

Only one grain carrying boat remained, and this was forced to run partially loaded because of the shallows. It survived only because carting corn from the railway to Lucy's Mill was even more difficult than steaming up the decaying Navigation.

For several years, the Great Western Railway had complete control of transport into Stratford, using the river, canal, tramway, and a new branch line connecting Stratford with Honeybourne, on the Evesham-Oxford section of the old OW&WR (see map page 68). This monopoly was broken only by the passing of an Act for an Evesham, Redditch and Stratford-upon-Avon Junction Railway, which offered a route between Evesham, Bidford and Stratford, competing with the river and also with the Evesham-Honeybourne-Stratford rail service of the Great Western. When its rival began to trade, the GWR ceased taking Avon tolls, and abandoned the river completely. Thus the end arrived, sometime in 1875.

Still convinced that they could ply a profitable trade on the river, if only it would be looked after as required in its Act of Parliament, the Avon's users declined to accept the abandonment, and took their fight to court.

The legislators of Victorian England had for some time been concerned that wealthy railway companies might purchase competing waterways specifically in order to close them, to eliminate competition in their area. Being generally opposed to such monopolist practices, because they would keep prices artificially high and stifle economic development, Parliament included in the 1873 Railway And Canal Traffic Act the statement:

> Every railway company owning or having the management of any canal or part of a canal shall at all times keep and maintain such canal . . . so that the whole . . . may at all times be kept open and Navigable for the use of all persons desirous to use and Navigate the same without any uneccessary hindrance, interruption or delay.

Any reasonable reading of the above would suggest that abandonment of the Avon was a contravention of the Act. Those who wished to continue to sail the river used this argument as a basis for preparation of a case against the mighty railway. Their complaint was stated by one of the traders, Foster Brothers:

> In the year 1859 a line of railway was constructed from Honeybourne to Stratford-upon-Avon, and this line subsequently became the property of the Great Western Railway Company. It therefore became, [Foster Brothers] declared, the interest of the railway company to cause the use of the Upper Avon Navigation to be discontinued and put an end to, in order that goods which would otherwise pass and be carried by river, should pass over the railways of the Great Western. Of the users of the river, they said 'these persons had suffered great inconvenience by the Upper Navigation ceasing to be navigable, and had been compelled to use the company's lines.'

Clearly, the Great Western had a case to answer. It chose to fight its ground by denying that it was ever the legal owner of the Navigation, thus exhonorating the company from any responsilibty for its well-being. In its first submission to the examining Judge, before the hearing itself, the railway company stated that the river had been abandoned prior to 1860, and had never been its problem. The railway dissociated itself from ownership due to Broughton's purchase, with the following argument, reported by a journalist present at the hearing;

> It was verbally arranged between the OW&WR and the then manager of the Stratford and Avon Canal Company, that this manager should purchase, in his own name, the Upper Avon Navigation, and the tolls and tonnage rates. This arrangement, which was *ultra vires*, was carried out, and the purchase money paid by the manager was repaid by the company to him, but no deed of conveyance was executed by the owners and proprietors transferring the tolls to the manager and no Act of Parliament was passed whereby the Navigation became vested in any of the railway companies, and the respondants submitted that they were not the owners and proprietors of the Navigation within the true intent meaning of the Act of Parliament . . . Besides . . . the receipts of tolls and tonnage rates was a condition precedent to, or at any rate, concurrent with the duty of keeping up the Navigation, and that the receipts of tolls and the rates had been duly abandoned and relinquished before the grievances alleged.

Challenging these remarks, the applicants said that the river had not been abandoned prior to 1860, being used before, during and after that year by the steamer *Bee* on her grain run (*see Chapter 10*). They also said, in defence of their claim that the railway had managed the river, that Broughton had taken tolls on

Grange lock and mill, Bidford, showing how much the Upper Avon locks had decayed by the time this drawing was made, about 40 years after abandonment.   *Charles Showell*

The remains of Lucy's staircase. Stratford, at the turn of the century, the drawing presumably showing the bottom of the two chambers. The spire on the left of the drawing is Holy Trinity Church.   *Charles Showell*

behalf of the OW&WR, and that later the GWR had itself received money, Messrs Hudson and Inns succeeding Broughton at the job of managing the Upper Avon.

On learning of the case made against it, but before the first sitting of the court, the GWR filed an amended answer, in which it presented a slightly different story. It alleged that in the late 1850s, the traders requested Broughton, as a private individual who just happened to be experienced in waterways management, to negotiate between it and the syndicate who owned the river. The alleged arrangement reached between Broughton and the traders was that, provided he could buy the navigation for less than £500, they would buy it from him for £200 more. The reason for this complicated scheme was not stated. *Acting for himself,* said the GWR, and having no power to act for the railway company, Broughton went ahead and bought the river, but received neither an Act of Conveyence nor his promised £200. The railway company's representative neglected to mention the quotation from its Board meeting, reproduced earlier in this chapter, which effectively contradicted all of this submission.

In their reply to this new version of the Great Western's Story, the applicants stressed that Broughton had most definitely been the agent of the OW&WR, and that in any case he had *taken tolls on the railway's behalf* when the purchase had been made. They denied having asked Broughton to negotiate on their behalf, though they had made him an offer for the river *after* he had purchased it, which he refused. This then was the background to the hearing, which opened on Friday 27th January, 1877.

The solicitor Powell, acting for the plaintiffs, professed that under the Act of 1751 the respondents were still the owners of the Navigation, as there had been no abandonment of tolls for the whole river (the Lower Avon was still demonstrably trading). They also said that even if this fact were open to doubt, the GWR took tolls and so were the managers under that Act. Statements were received on the first day from Foster Bros and Jacob Rice (carriers), Joseph Neal and Jack Spragg (Bidford boat owners), E.O. Hancock (Evesham miller) and Mrs Perrott who was still an owner of the Lower Avon; all of these testified the river's importance. The hearing was then adjourned.

On Saturday, Powell handed over accounts and minute books of the OW&WR, and some toll tickets sporting the name of that company, to underline that the railway must have taken river tolls, and closed his case. Replying, the GWR again denied that it had ever owned the Navigation, and pointed out that it could not have taken it over without an Act of Parliament even in the sense of the 1873 Act (section 17). Further, it emphasised that ceasing to take tolls implied a cessation of responsibility under the 1751 Avon Act (*see Chapter Four*). Its main witness was Mr Sherriff who had been manager of the OW&WR. He said,

> In 1859 Mr Broughton, the manager of the canal . . . said that the canal, the Company's property [referring to the OW&WR], was being damaged by the state of the Upper Avon Navigation and, acting for the Railway Company . . . said that any assistance which the railway could give would be given.

In reply to a question, Sherriff then said that he had instructed Broughton to subsidise the Upper Avon from the coffers of the Stratford Canal. The minutes of the Directors of the OW&WR for January 1859 were then called to the witnesses attention. They read:

> Re the purchase of the Upper Avon Navigation - Mr Whately having agreed to accept the sum of £300 for this purchase, the matter was referred to Mr Sherriff.

Sherriff, when questioned, denied all knowledge of this. Pressed further, he was asked to give an explanation of the OW&WR toll tickets produced by the applicants, dating from the time that he was manager (1860). No explanation was forthcoming. Before the hearing was adjourned, printed toll receipts headed 'Great Western Railway Company' were shown, as proof that the GWR itself was taking tolls and managing the river in accordance with the Act of 1873.

When the case reopened on Monday, some correspondence between Messrs New, Price and Garrard (agents of the traders), Mr Pidcock (solicitor to the OW&WR) and Mr Broughton was presented, demonstrating that the railway company had indeed bought the Navigation. Finally, it was pointed out that the GWR dared not call the most obvious witness, Mr Broughton himself. Judgement was postponed until St Valentine's day, 1877.

To sum up - the river traders had receipts from both the OW&WR and the GWR to prove that the railway companies were taking tolls, correspondence between parties to prove that the OW&WR bought the Upper Avon, and also sworn statements from river users. The Great Western had two stories (the original submission and the amendment), both of which denied ownership of, and responsibility for, the waterway. Unfortunately for the Avon traders, the railway company was in a strict legal sense quite correct, because it could not have acquired it without an Act of Parliament. It had, in fact, been accepting money for the use of navigation which it did not own! This legal loophole was a gift to the GWR, and Sir Fredrick Peel gave the predictable judgement; the Great Western won the case, but had to pay half the costs, and bear heavy criticism from the Judge.

That day, in the dry and dusty atmosphere of a court hearing, the fate of the beautiful and peaceful Upper Avon was sealed. Its ancient locks and weirs, which had meant so much for the growth and propserity of its towns, were left to crumble into the soft river mud, and the upper river began to return to its old, unmanaged state.

Chapter Ten

Fighting Back

Although the Upper Avon Navigation had been lost, trade continued downstream of Evesham. The opening of the Gloucester and Berkeley Canal had improved shipping in the Lower Severn, the new locks at Tewkesbury and Gloucester deepened water higher up the Severn, and Tewkesbury still handled a large freight traffic. Mills at Evesham and Nafford received grain by water several times per month, and some building materials also travelled in barges. Coal, however, was carried by rail alone. Barges numbered about one every two days, travelling up from Tewkesbury. Some were still bow-hauled, but the appearance in 1862, of the steamer *Bee*, her barge *Lorie*, and later her sister steamer *Wasp* (all owned by Jacob Rice and Co., Offenham) heralded a new era in shipping. The steamers each towed up to three dumb barges about three times per month, their introduction coinciding with the last years of the Upper Avon. Soon almost all of the trade on the river was in the hands of Rice, though he faced stiff competition from the railways.

The toll receipts of the years 1860 to 1902 are shown on page 76. The Worcester and Birmingham was making a loss on the Navigation, due to maintenance costs, and, and although its losses were declining, being £112, £87 and £7 in the years 1870-72, the company tried to sell its whole canal system to the Midland Railway. It referred the question of the renewal of the Lower Avon lease to that company, who advised against it. The main reason for the lease was, after all, to compete with traffic descending the Avon from Stratford, which had now stopped. Thus when the lease expired on 29th September 1872, the Lower Avon passed back into independent control. Barges continued to travel its waters, albeit less frequently than in times past.

Considering that the railways had been the death of the Upper Avon, it is a little ironic that they should have been instrumental in generating new river traffic from the close of the century. Pleasure boating had been becoming increasingly popular since its beginnings on the Norfolk broads in the 1870s. Cheap rail transport opened up towns such as Stratford-upon-Avon to the nascent tourist industry, and pleasure boats began to be more prominent on the waters of the Avon. Quiller Couch, who wrote his *Warwickshire Avon* in 1891, wrote that the river was crowded with pleasure boats at Stratford. By 1898, passenger craft were making daily trips from Tewkesbury to Evesham in the summer. Of course, because the toll system was still that laid down in 1751, this new traffic generated no revenue and might actually have raised maintenance costs, but the increased use of the river gave hope to some public-spirited individuals who wished to see the Avon fully navigable again.

In 1895, Mr George Hunt (the then Mayor of Evesham) called a conference of representatives of the municipalitites of Stratford-upon-Avon, Evesham and Tewkesbury, and any others who were interested in the matter, to discuss the state of the river. The following resolution was passed:

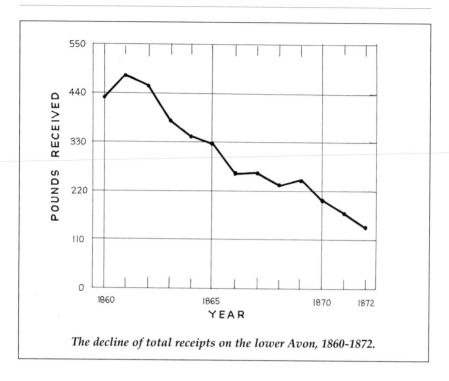

The decline of total receipts on the lower Avon, 1860-1872.

The steam tug *Bee* in Strensham lock.

Charles Showell

That the members of the conference being of the opinion that the restoration of the Upper Avon would conduce to the public interests hereby form themselves into a committee with the power to add to their number, to communicate with the Public Authorities and Trading Companies and Associations concerned or interested in the Navigation, and the Board of Trade, with a view to ascertain whether they will co-operate in any such measures as may be necessary for effecting such restoration.

The committee devoted a great deal of time to the formulation of a scheme, and obtained the general assent of the Boroughs of Stratford, Evesham, Tewkesbury and the city of Gloucester, subject to the approval of details. The County Council of Gloucester required a properly worked out estimate of costs. A 'thoroughly well qualified engineer', Mr G.W. Keeling of the Sharpness New Docks Co., reckoned the cost to be £10,000. In February 1897, a formal report was made to several local authorities. It set out the proposed plan of action:

1. A canal Trust should be formed to carry out the restoration of the Upper Avon, so as to constitute a waterway for through traffic from the Severn at Tewkesbury to the Stratford Canal by a provisional order . . .
2. That the canal trust be authorised to raise by mortgage of the revenue of the Upper Avon Navigation the cost of restoration and incidental expenses . . .
3. As a matter of suggestion only it was submitted that the following bodies might contribute to the guarantee as under . . .

The Sharpness New Docks Co	$\frac{1}{20}$
County Council of Gloucester	$\frac{1}{20}$
County Council of Worcestershire	$\frac{2}{20}$
County Council of Warwickshire	$\frac{5}{20}$
Town Council of Tewkesbury	$\frac{1}{20}$
Town Council of Evesham	$\frac{4}{20}$
Town Council of Stratford	$\frac{5}{20}$
City Council of Gloucester	$\frac{1}{20}$

4. That a restoration committee should be formed by guaranteeing bodies, in proportion to their respective shares . . .

These proposals were widely reported in the local press of the area, and the response seemed warm. It was pointed out that even if no revenue was generated by the river, the burden on local rates would be very low, being 1d. in the pound at Evesham and Stratford, and less than 1d. in £100 elsewhere. The approval of all parties except the county councils was obtained. In order to decide its response to the scheme, Worcester County Council held an enquiry on 23rd April, 1897. The opponents were, as in the time of William Sandys, mostly riparian owners, who had organised themselves (with Slater Son and Gibbs as their solicitors) in a meeting at the Red Horse Hotel in Stratford on 11th December, 1896. The main complaint was that riparian rights would be damaged, a claim which was attacked by the *Stratford Herald* two days later:

[It is] perfectly certain that no riparian rights would be invaded, as the proposal was only intended to restore the river to the condition it occupied in its palmy days. No opposition, therefore, to thwart the scheme could possibly be attended with success.

In general, the report of the meeting seemed to be in favour of the scheme, but

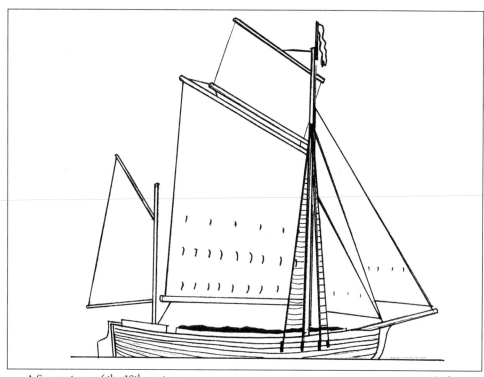

A Severn trow of the 19th century. *Author*

The ford at the Fish and Anchor, Offenham. *Author*

the final recommendation of the Council was as follows:

> Your Committee . . . felt that they could not recommend to the Council to support a scheme that only deals with the Upper Avon and not the Avon as a whole. While they think that the council should be prepared to respond favourably . . . they consider that the present scheme is too crude and incomplete . . .

On 13th July, 1897, the finance committee of Warwickshire County Council received a deputation of nine gentlemen who represented the municipalities of Stratford and Evesham, the Sharpness New Docks Co. and Henry de Salis (Director of the canal carrying company Fellows Moreton and Clayton). These men spoke in favour of the scheme. However, the council had been making its own cost estimates, which were rather higher than that of the proponents, and they replied:

> In view of the wide difference which exists as to the possible cost of the scheme and of the improbability - according to past experience - of the undertaking proving renumerative . . . the Council do at present take no action in the matter.

The inaction caught the scheme in a stalemate, and it foundered.

The reporting of the above events by local newpapers created a public interest in the river, and the general level of impatience with the impasse grew until in 1899, under the guidance of Mr William Smith and a few other spirited locals, the River Avon Improvement Association (RAIA) was formed. It advocated restoration of the river by voluntary means, and even started dredging the river near Evesham in demonstration of its seriousness. As the century turned, the river gained a growing group of friends. Having been approached by the RAIA, the town council of Evesham lent its support to the restoration scheme and they applied to the County Council of Worcester to set about

> . . . the improvement and repair of that part of the Avon Navigation and highway over the River Avon above Evesham, which lies in the County of Worcester, so as to provide facilities for river barge traffic, small steamers and pleasure boats.

One of the hallmarks of a committee, especially one in public office, is that its left hand can be blissfully unaware of what its right hand is doing. Evesham Town Council demonstrated this trait superbly during the time when it supported the restoration scheme; they built an illegal ford at 'Fish and Anchor', and blocked the Navigation completely. The ford, being well built and piled, restricted draught to a matter of inches and made it impossible for a vessel larger than a canoe to pass it (indeed it is now used as an obstacle on a yearly charity raft race).

As a result of pressure from the Evesham Town Council (presumably the same individuals who had passed the plans for the ford!), the County Council held two enquiries of 22nd and 27th July, 1903. Evidence for greatly increased demand for pleasure boats was used to add support to the restoration, though this made riparian owners even less happy about the opening of the river. The main conclusions of the enquiries were as follows:

1. The commissioners of the enquiry agreed that the opening would be beneficial to the community, but would probably not be revenue-earning.
2. Pleasure traffic was at the moment damaging to the remains of the Upper Avon, as it was totally unregulated (a point stressed by Riparian owners).
3. The Commissioner disagreed with the opponents to the restoration, who claimed that it would increase flooding. Floods, they said, would be less likely, and anyway levels were legally fixed in George II's Act.
4. The conclusion was that the scheme would be cheap but not self-supporting, and the council was recommended to proceed.

An interesting footnote said that the new ford at 'Fish and Anchor' was an illegal obstruction, and that any of the King's Subjects had the right to remove it. Nobody did.

When the recommendations reached the County Council itself, on 14th September, it went to the vote proposed by J. Willis Bund and the Chairman. Opposition was on the grounds of cost, and that the main justification of the scheme was for pleasure craft which brought little revenue to the area (the potential economic value of tourism was not then appreciated). Unfortunately, two members of the council known to favour the scheme were not able to attend the meeting, and it was defeated by exactly two votes.

Public interest in the restoration continued undiminished for a while, and in 1905 a book entitled *The River Avon- Why Its Navigation Should Be Restored and How It May Be Done* was published by the River Avon Improvement Association. To make their case, its authors compared the state of British inland navigation with that of European canals, which were being improved constantly. They argued that the fact that Thomas Cook (the famous holiday tour company) dealt with Avon Boat trips from Evesham to Tewkesbury, was excellent evidence for growing demand for recreational use of the waterways, and pointed out that the provision of recreational facilities was a *legal obligation* of local authorities. These and other arguments were put nearly 40 years later with even stronger force by the nascent Inland Waterways Association, with much more success. The book resulted in no real action, and although members of the RAIA continued to write to the press for years afterwards, their publication was, with hindsight, the last serious attempt to get the river reopened. At no time in the next 60 years did it seem as likely that the Avon would be navigable throughout as it did in 1903, when two absent voters made all the difference.

Chapter Eleven

Sad Locks and Happy Tourists

After its brief hopes of revival at the turn of the century, the navigation slipped deeper into decay. Where once large freighters carried heavy loads of coal up-river to Stratford, even punts found the going difficult. In 1909, the river enthusiast A.G. Bradley wrote, 'Swollen by the entry of the Stour near Stratford, it [the Avon] runs henceforward a good brimming stream, where in many parts two . . . boats can row abreast.'

In the same waters where little boats could sometimes row two abreast, *Bee* had once towed three laden barges!

An interest in books on travel and exploration prompted several authors to write about journeys on the Avon, leaving modern readers with valuable descriptive material. Much of this documents the decay of navigation works. Recalling his early visits to the Avon, one writer said:

> When I first came down the Avon from Stratford- it was, I think, about 1890 or 1891 - the process of disintegration had been going on for a long time. There were ruins and vestiges of locks and weirs and lashers all the way down, but none was capable of being used until you came to Evesham and even below that they were in the last stages of decreptitude.

At Lucy's weir,

> . . . we found no lock at all, but only crumbling walls with the river running through them like a sluice.

A keen canoeist, he made a journey down the whole of the river in such a craft:

> It was an exciting trip, and Avon will never be like that again, so I am glad I saw the last stage of her crumbling navigation. The shades of Sandys and Yarranton must, I should imagine, haunt the sites of these dead locks.

Quiller Couch, who undertook a similar trip, wrote:

> Till Evesham be passed we shall meet with no barges, but with shallows, dismantled locks, broken down weirs to be shot, and sound ones to be pulled over that will give us excitement enough, and toil too.

He also describes the ruins; for example,

> By Weston our remembrance keeps a picture - a broken lock and weir, and islet or two heavy with purple loosestrife, a swan bathing in the channel between . . .

Not all was decay. The tourist industry continued its exuberant growth even on the Upper Avon, where traffic was of course restricted to the short lengths

The waterfront of Edwardian Stratford, showing how busy even parts of the river separated from the main navigation could become. The large building in the background is the Royal Shakespeare Theatre that burned down in March 1926. *Stratford Record Office*

An advertisement for one of Byrd's steamers, *Lilybyrd*. She must have been crowded when carrying her maximum permitted 120 persons!

SALOON STEAMER "LILYBYRD."
Registered to carry 120.

OPEN FOR ENGAGEMENTS
Any distance on the Avon.

DAILY TRIPS.
Terms Moderate.

between ruined locks. Demand for boating in Stratford itself was enough to justify occasional dredging of the pound above the weir by traction engine. In July 1897 the local newspaper ran an advertisment which illustrates a typical craft used for day-trippers. It was for the steam boat *Zanita*, which was described as 'a good traveller, and perfectly free from vibration; and being of shallow draught can trace the river for a long distance upstream.' Bidford, too, had a pleasure boat operator in the shape of W.H. Holland, who operated more than 50 small craft before the collapse of Cleeve weir. His business was also connected with other changes in the Avon's economy; many local water-mills had closed in favour of a few large steam flour-processors in ports and industrial towns, and the old mill at Cleeve Prior was converted into tea-rooms. Holland made a good living carrying day-trippers from Bidford to the Cleeve tea rooms for many years, until the old mill was destroyed by fire in the 1930s.

Because the Lower Avon was still in reasonable condition, the bulk of the trip boat traffic was concentrated here, especially at Evesham. As early as 1879, the boat owner Charles Byrd advertised:

> In calling attention to those having the management of excursions, picnics or school parties, Charles Byrd begs to announce that he is the proprietor of the *Golden Fleece* Steam Pleasure Boat Plying to all parts. To accommodate 150 persons. Also a steam pleasure yacht, to accommodate about 30 persons

By 1900, Evesham alone had four companies (Byrds, Spragg, Malins and Groves) operating pleasure boats. During the summer months, trippers from the Black Country (known locally as 'the Dudleys') would pour out of packed excursion trains and on to Evesham's streets: '. . . Evesham had become a mecca for train loads of day trippers . . . river trips on the *Lilybyrd* and *Diamond Queen* from Byrds' landing stage . . . were increasing in popularity'.

With an expanding market, other boats were bought or built. By the 1930s, Evesham's boats included *Lily Byrd*, *Hurley*, *Jubilee*, *Diamond Queen*, *King George V*, *Tagus* and *Gaiety*. Each has its own particular history, but in these pages, their last survivor, *Gaiety*, shall speak for them all. The 72 ft, 70 ton steamer began life in 1887, in the boatyard of Edwin Clark and Co. at the then substantial inland port of Brimscombe, near Stroud. Built of closely-framed riveted steel, her hull took over a year to complete, and she was launched in 1889. Her first, unpowered, voyage was along the Stroudwater Canal and up the Gloucester and Sharpness Canal to Gloucester, where she was equipped with her steam plant by the Sissons engineering works. Bearing the name *Oxford*, she then travelled back through the Stroudwater and Thames and Severn Canals, to her new home on the Thames, where she was operated as a trip boat by Salters. Here, the *Oxford* spent the next 30 years of her life, carrying loads of up to 150 tourists in what was the hey-day of Thames Elegance.

In 1929, Salters offered Oxford for sale, and the Evesham boat operator Sammy Groves bought her for use on the Avon at Evesham, and changed her name to *Gaiety*. Her journey back to the Severn system was much harder than her emigration from it in 1889, because the old Thames and Severn Canal had fallen into complete ruin. Had she been a narrow-boat, she could have travelled

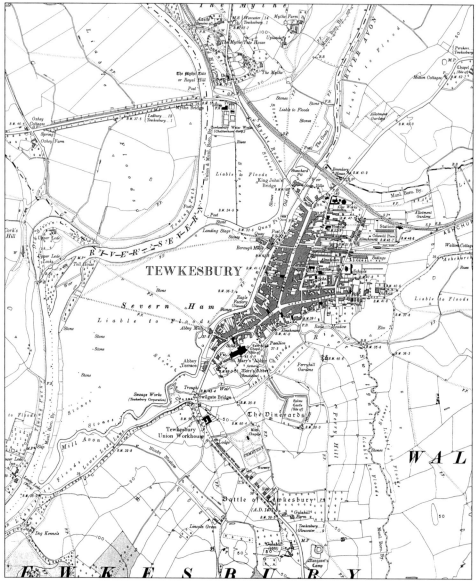

Tewkesbury showing the rather complicated confluence of the rivers Avon and Severn, which join at two places. The navigable connection is through Tewkesbury lock, which takes vessels down to the 'Old Avon' channel and into the Severn. Another part of the Avon, the 'Mill Avon' (navigable as far as Abbey Mills) meets the Severn much further south, thus creating the Island of Severn Ham. Just downstream of Tewkesbury lock is Quay Pool (*illustrated on page 90*). By the 1920s the quay and Healings Mill beside it were served by a siding from the railway that offered services to Gloucester, Evesham and Stratford upon Avon. The site of the railway's viaduct across the Avon is now occupied by a large marina complex with basins off the 'Old Avon' below and the main line of the navigation above Tewkesbury weir. *Reproduced from the 6", 1924 Ordnance Survey Map*

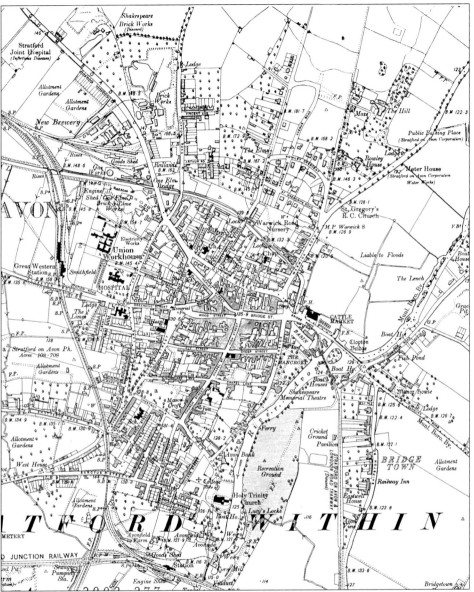

Stratford-upon-Avon in 1920. Through navigation of the river was impossible by this date, the locks being in ruins, but the 5 places on the map marked 'Boat House' attest its popularity for local pleasure craft. The Bathing Place is evidence of another popular leisure pursuit (no longer encouraged). Lucy's Mill had generated the last major freight traffic on the Upper Avon, had by this time acquired a rail link to the Stratford & Midland Junction Railway's station. The canal was still in very occasional use, and the interchange sidings with the closed tramway are still marked although the second canal basin has already been filled in to form Bancroft Gardens. Andrew Yarranton's New Town (*see* Chapter 3) would have been sited just to the north of Bridge Town.

Reproduced from the 6", 1920 Ordnance Survey Map

The remains of Lucy's locks, Stratford about 1900.   *J. Garrett*

Alabama, Gaiety's sister, being built at Brimscombe.   *E. Clark*

Gaiety in steam days cruising through Evesham.   *S. Groves & Co.*

The Mill Avon, Tewkesbury, at the turn of the century, with Tewkesbury Abbey in the background.

Charles Showell

The same view today illustrating how the waterfront has changed to provide moorings for cruisers small enough to turn in the narrow Mill Avon.

Author

from the Thames to the Avon via the Oxford, Grand Union, (Northern) Stratford, and Worcester and Birmingham canals, but *Gaiety's* broad beam barred her from this route. The only inland passage available was via the Kennet and Avon Navigation, which made use of navigable rivers and canal sections to connect Reading on the Thames with the Bristol Channel. Although it was technically open, this waterway was in an extremely poor state of repair, and *Gaiety's* difficult 213 mile passage earned her a mention in the *Daily Telegraph*! Eleven days after leaving the Thames, Groves' new boat reached the Avon, and following a difficult journey through its silted-up locks, she was greeted on 21st March by cheering crowds of spectators at Evesham.

The yard in which *Gaiety* found herself was a busy one, operating a fleet of other steamers, punts, rowing boats and a busy café, and employing up to 11 men in the summer. Her usual skipper was Mr G. Spencer, who came from Gloucester but lodged in Evesham in summer. Most journeys made were either short ones, as far as Chadbury lock, or day-trips to Fladbury and back, but newspaper advertisments of the time suggest that longer journeys were made before the locks became too difficult to use.

For her first few years on the Avon, the launch retained her original steam plant (serviced, incidentally, by the Bomford and Evershed works, described for posterity in L.T.C. Rolt's *Landscape with Machines*). Later, though, it was replaced by a small diesel unit which proved more economical, as well as cleaner. The other steamers in the Evesham fleet left the river over the years, either being sold, wrecked, or broken up. *Gaiety* continued to run until the late 1980s, making the trip from Evesham to Chadbury weir several times a day in the summer, and becoming a well-known feature of the river, her fine lines beloved of tourists, and her sharp prow feared by scullers of the local rowing and sailing clubs.

The elegant river-boat made her last journey on the waters of the Avon in December 1987, when she was lifted from them by crane and transferred to a 60 ft low-loader. The lorry took her, in a few hours, along the journey which had taken 11 days in 1929, and returned her to the Thames after her 58 year exile. Now located at Richmond, Surrey, the converted steamer continues to give pleasure to those who seek it on the peaceful waters of a river.

Many of the voyages were enlivened by on-board entertainment. Twice a year a Cardiff choir would travel on the *Hurley*, entertaining not only her passengers but also the crowds who gathered on the banks to hear them. These long trips would have been very interesting to any waterway enthusiast, with the original features of the Avon, such as rounded lock chambers and the watergates still in use. The latter were the source of long delays in traffic, as the pound of the river below the next upstream lock took up to an hour to fill, and they could also be hazardous, as recounted by Charles Showell:

> On one occasion when I was staying in the neighbourhood [of Fladbury] a rather comical incident occurred. One evening a large pleasure steamer, the *Lily* of Evesham, passed up [through the watergate at Cropthorne] with a party of about 30 on board. She passed through the gate, which was then closed, and twenty minutes or half an hour later the water would rise enough for her to proceed on her homeward journey to

Healings Mill, Tewkesbury, at the turn of the century. The three trows are typical of craft trading on the Severn system at that time, and brought grain to the large mill behind them. Because the mill was built to be accessible from the river below Tewkesbury weir, its boats did not have to pass through Tewkesbury lock and so paid no tolls to the Avon. The bridge in the centre of the drawing, the 'locomotive bridge', crosses the Avon at the higher level (above Tewkesbury lock and weir, which are directly behind the artist). The route under the locomotive bridge, the 'Mill Avon', leads past the Abbey to another mill, while the main line of the navigation heads in the opposite direction (behind the artist). *Charles Showell*

A similar view today (trees now screen the exact original viewpoint). Healings Mill, modernised in 1975, still uses water transport, grain being brought up the Severn in the motor barges *Tirley* and *Chaceley*, which were originally built for coal traffic in the North East. Three smaller and older barges also moored at the mill, *Deerhurst, Apperley,* and *Bushley,* are at present unused.

Author

This postcard depicting Marie Corelli and the gondola she imported to Stratford from Venice, was one of a series that caused such offence to the novelist that she attempted to sue the publisher (without success). It was issued around 1906.   *Hugh Mcknight Collection*

Miranda, a cruiser hired in 1938 from Bathursts of Tewkesbury by Tom Rolt and his fiancée Angela Orred. The boat is lying across the diamond of Wyre lock.   *Sonia Rolt*

Evesham. Immediately after, a skiff came up, shortly followed by our boat. The occupants of the skiff proceeded to open the sluices, although they knew that *Lily* could not have passed into Fladbury Lock. By the time we arrived the water was down and the gate reopened, so through we went, the other crew following. Presently a man came running from Fladbury, excitedly shouting 'Ay, You've done a fine thing, you have! You've broken the *Lily's* back'. We referred him to the other men who, with becoming modesty, were hanging back . . . the *Lily* was stuck on the sill of the lock . . . where she was destined to remain for some time.

It is possible that Showell was confused over the identity of the boat, as Jack Langston, a steerer of Grove's steamers, remembers that *Lily Byrd* was renamed *Enterprise* and sold as a houseboat, while *Jubilee* was wrecked at Fladbury.

As well as large pleasure boats, the river was crammed with punts and skiffs during the summer months. Some of the weirs were fitted with special rollers to permit the passage of small pleasure boats, so great was their number, and the remains of these rollers can still be seen at Evesham and Chadbury locks. To illustrate a typical Avon scene, here is Garrett's description of Tewkesbury:

There are numerous people on the landing stage; the day is fine and several companies of friends have come into Tewkesbury for a water picnic on the Avon and this gathering consists of pleasure-seekers waiting to get afloat in rowing boats, or in one of the little steam launches to be hired. The bright colours of cotton and silk . . . and flowers and feather, in blouse and shirt and hat and parasol; the water flashing with reflections of the sun between green banks, and the voices and light laughter of the people make a gay and joyous scene.

Stratford was even more gay with the laughter of tourists, some of whom had made use of local hostelries to achieve their merry state. According to the local press, several subsequently met their deaths in the tangles of weeds beneath its inviting surface. In 1895, the river was so busy that a sculler drowned after having capsized while trying to avoid the mass of other boats! A few intrepid canoeists made the journey along the ruined Upper Avon navigation and left us with impressions of the river like those quoted at the beginning of this chapter. Small craft also made the journey upstream to Warwick, although they were impeded by booms erected across the river by the owners of Charlecote House near Hampton Lucy. The townspeople themselves turned to the river for recreation, and both Stratford and Evesham formed rowing clubs which still produce the occasional Olympic oarsman. One of the most remarkable craft to travel the Stratford Pound in those days was *The Dream*, a genuine gondola owned by the novelist Marie Corelli, who had imported both the boat and a gondalier from Venice! The incongruous craft became famous enough to be the subject of a postcard that resulted in legal action by Miss Corelli, who felt that she was not being portrayed in a favourable enough light (*see page 91*).

The practice of hiring out boats for long cruises dates back to the 1870s, when boatyards on the Thames and Norfolk Broads began the holiday hire business. Later, this spread to other stretches of water, and on the Lower Avon a few enterprising yards hired out motor cruisers for weeks. In his autobiography,

L.T.C. Rolt (one of the original leaders of the waterways restoration movement) recalls using one to find out whether he and his wife would enjoy living on a boat. Their experiences on the navigation did nothing to discourage them, and their subsequent travels have passed into waterway folklore and history.

Though it provided much pleasure to pleasure seekers, the Avon gave little joy to its proprietors or remaining carriers. During the World War I, the condition of the river deteriorated, and takings dropped. In 1917, Jacob Rice announced the sale of *Bee* because the mills which she had served had closed, and the river was in a poor state. From 1918 only one boat still ran regularly, taking loads of grain to Pershore mill.

Pressure from the residents of the area, and the remaining members of the RAIA, prompted the County Councils of Gloucester, Worcestershire and Warwickshire to form an Avon Navigation Joint Committee in 1919, which resurrected the scheme which had been defeated in 1903, and appointed a subcommittee to submit it to the Ministry of Transport. Early in 1920, the Government set up the Neville Chamberlain Committee on inland waterways. The Chairman of the joint committee, Mr Jeffrey New, was called to give evidence to them. The original, modest plan stood a good chance of success, but the Joint Committee had decided to submit a plan whereby 100 ton barges would be able to navigate all of the way to Warwick, and an inclined plane would lift them on to the Warwick and Napton Canal. The latter was still a narrow waterway, but the committee assumed that it would be widened; years later, as part of the Grand Union system, it was indeed rebuilt to 14 ft gauge. The estimated cost of the Avon improvement was a staggering £230,000, and needless to say the scheme came to nothing.

As these negotiations were taking place, the toll of the elements was being felt ever more acutely, both in damage to works and lost revenue because of flooding. In 1921, Evesham's Town Clerk wrote to Mr H.B. Harrison (a Pershore solicitor acting for the Avon proprietors), saying 'The Evesham Corporation definitely suggest that the river is not kept in a fit state for Navigation'. The Corporation had always made use of the proximity of their gasworks to the river to use boats for disposal of tar. William Butler of Bristol had for some years taken a boat just above Evesham Lock, collected the tar, and then taken it on to Bristol. This was no longer possible, and when the letter was written, 'with great difficulty and additional expense this tar has to be sent by rail'. Butler himself wrote to Harrison, explaining that Wyre Lock (a nominal 4 ft 6 in. deep) was so silted that a freight boat could not pass it.

While the lock at Wyre Piddle had been the final straw for Butler's boats, the state of all of the locks had long been dubious. For example, in 1891 the condition of Evesham lock was described by Bliss:

It was just [usable] when I first came in 1891, but could only be opened by means of some extrordinary contrivance of derricks and pulleys and winches that looked exactly like one of Mr Heath Robinson's pictures.

Faced with sights of locks such as these, the good men of Evesham Town Council decided to perform their own small survey of the Lower Avon, to see what needed to be put right. Among their suggestions to Harrison, were stopping leaks in Tewkesbury lock, dredging Strensham lock cut, clearing overhanging trees, replacing the gates at Nafford and repairing the bridge there, replacing Pensham water-gate, dredging Wyre lock 2 ft 6 in. to attain nominal levels, and repairing Wyre and Chadbury locks! Complaints and suggestions were also forthcoming from pleasure boat operators. For example, Bathursts of Tewkesbury (operating at least one river cruise per week in summer, and owning four passenger steamers) complained that even his comparatively shallow draughted craft could not pass Wyre.

Faced with these problems, and a severe shortage of money with which to rectify them, Harrison asked to be released from his position as the representative of the Lower Avon Company. Its remaining shareholders appointed Messrs Perrott-Stimson and Fisher to see that the river was repaired. Unsure of the extent of decay in their waterway, they commissioned the engineer J.W. Smith to conduct a full survey. His report, which was in broad agreement with the comments of Evesham Town Council, was not encouraging. Because of the chronic lack of money for the river, almost all of the lock gates dated from the 1880s, and those at Nafford, Wyre, Pensham water-gate and Cropthorne water-gate were in extremely urgent need of repair.

At this point, rather dismayed at the costs of maintenance of their concern, the Lower Avon Company's shareholders attempted to sell it to the Sharpness New Docks Company, but failed. Unwilling to give up, they elected to purchase the river outright, and to rebuild it as well as they could manage. They formed a limited company, and succeeded in raising £4,000 through debentures. With this, they purchased the interests of the Perrott trust, and a further £2,300 was spent on repairs over the next six years.

During the 1930s, the river again worsened, and takings fell. Examination of the account book of Tewkesbury lock reveals that, with the exception of the grain motor barge *Pisgah*, freight ceased to be carried at all, and the only takings were from lock fees of passenger vessels, which were exempt, under the Avon Act, from paying tonnage. In the early 1940s the river became completely unnavigable above Pershore. At the end of the war the works were in a state of near collapse, and it seemed to all concerned with it, that the 300 year history of the Avon Navigation was about to end.

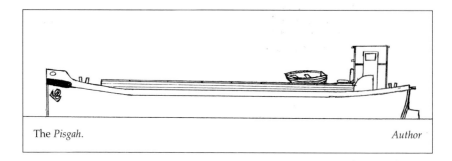

The *Pisgah*.   *Author*

Chapter Twelve

The Rebirth of the Lower Avon

In 1945, just as World War II was drawing to a close, an Evesham Alderman by the name of John Whitehouse decided to attempt a rescue of the nearly moribund Lower Avon. Realising that the navigation's situation was desperate, he borrowed enough money to purchase 999 shares in the Lower Avon Navigation Company. As the new owner of the river, he became the proud possessor of all navigation rights, seven dilapidated locks and a rickety old wooden lock-keeper's hut at Tewkesbury. Perhaps because it carried so little traffic, the Avon escaped nationalisation in 1948 and remained in private ownership. Although Whitehouse clearly had every intention of maintaining the river in the best state he could, the expense of restoration was far too great for a private individual of relatively modest means, and its condition continued to deteriorate until 1949, when the lock at Strensham was becoming impassable. The collapse of this lock would have disconnected almost all of the river from the Severn, and thus meant its final closure to all traffic except rowing boats and punts.

Help was obviously needed, and as it happened the timing of John Whitehouse's attempted rescue was perfect for gaining the interest and support of others. Due largely to the publication of *Narrow Boat* by L.T.C. Rolt, the plight of the ancient inland navigations had reached the conciousness of the public. In 1946, Tom Rolt, Robert Aickman and a few other visionary individuals formed the Inland Waterways Association (IWA), to campaign for the development, retention and restoration of inland waterways. In Aickman's words, the Association advocated that they should,

> . . . exploit navigation in all its functions and potentialities, including commercial carrying, pleasure boating, water supply, land drainage and angling . . . There should be no more abandonments or closures under any circumstances, but, instead, at a later date, a drive for re-opening certain rivers and canals . . .

Membership increased rapidly in the early years as waterway enthusiasts and freight carriers rallied under the sword on the IWA's pennant, and vigorous action was taken in order that the waterways should be protected. Though not the first attempt to save navigations by volunteer action (the Avon itself was the subject of an earlier campaign, recounted in previous chapters), the efforts of the nascent IWA were to change the direction of management of Britain's waterways. The IWA's first serious attempt at restoration of a complete near-derelict waterway, the Basingstoke Canal, met with difficulties so severe that the canal was not re-opened until 1991 (even now, the uppermost reaches remain derelict). The title of the first waterway to be reopened by the new volunteers fell to the Lower Avon, and its success set the pattern for at least another 40 years of development.

The Lower Avon Navigation's restoration has its deepest roots in a 1949

LANT working party at Strensham lock. On the lock gate near the middle of the picture, is an example of pre-war Avon paddle gear. The men are placing stop-planks at the ends of the chamber, to act as a temporary dam. *Mrs E. Barwell*

Wyre lock under restoration in 1954. The chamber has already been dredged and the gates are now receiving attention. This was the only lock to remain diamond-shaped after restoration. *Mrs E. Barwell*

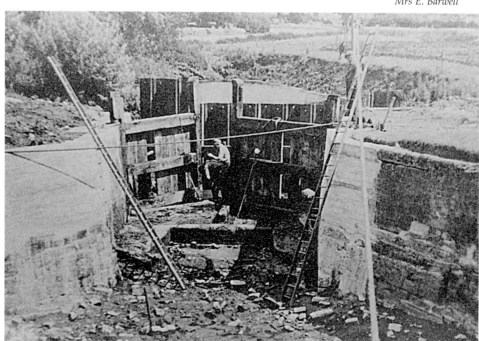

boating holiday during which C. Douglas Barwell, a Birmingham copper tube manufacturer and a member of the Midlands branch of the IWA, tried to navigate Whitehouse's Lower Avon. He had already made the journey years ago in a canoe built by his father, but this time he attempted it in his cruiser *North Star*. He succeeded in reaching Pershore, but on the return journey Nafford lock gates leaked so much that they had to be repaired with planks borrowed from a local farmer before they could be used! Inspired by his journey, and concerned that in a short while nobody would be able to repeat it, Barwell suggested the formation of an Avon sub-committee of the IWA Midlands branch, to investigate the possibility of restoration of the waterway. Its first meeting took place on 18th December, 1949, the energetic Barwell being elected Chairman.

Members of the sub-committee, particularly Robert Aickman and Douglas Barwell, spent much time visiting local towns and drumming up support for the restoration project. Especially important to the campaign were the

This photograph, dated 1950, shows the state of the locks taken over by LANT. As well as the obvious defects in the gates, many locks had problems with the masonry of the lock chambers themselves and required substantial rebuilding. *Mrs E. Barwell*

A cruiser using the restored Strensham lock in the 1990s.

remaining boatyards on the river, such as Bathursts in Tewkesbury who hired out a fleet of 2-, 4-, 6- and 8-berth cruisers (about 30 in all) for the Severn and Avon. Generally the response was very encouraging; the Avon remained a beautiful river, but if the weirs were to be allowed to fail much of it would have reverted to a muddy and reed-choked stream. The prospect of preventing this fate attracted support even from those who did not wish to explore the navigation by boat.

In January 1950, the Lower Avon sub-committee had gained enough strength to be able to contemplate taking over the navigation, and Barwell purchased it for the committee (with his own funds) for £1,438. Now that it had gained control of the navigation, the next priority of the group was to raise sufficient finances to assure its preservation. To this end, it sought the tax advantages of registration as a Charitable Trust, an objective which was achieved on 1st August, 1950.

Even today, when the country is richly blessed with railway, waterway and industrial societies with years of experience in the field, the starting and running of a new group can be daunting. The founders of the Lower Avon Navigation Trust (LANT) had no precedents on which to rely. They were true pioneers in the waterways field, and the age of amateur railway restoration was yet to arrive (L.T.C. Rolt left the IWA to begin the pioneering Talyllyn Railway restoration in 1951). With a few minor exceptions, the history of attempts to restoration of transport routes (as opposed to individual vessels and vehicles) was full of failure, and little expert advice was available.

The work facing the LANT committee could be divided up into several areas. The most obvious was fund-raising; lack of money had caused the river to deteriorate, and lack of money had so far prevented its restoration. Another necessity was the acquisition of new members, both to swell the Trust's coffers, and to provide volunteer navvies who were needed for rebuilding work. The ownership of the navigation also carried responsibilities to river users, and the Trust had to consider the best ways to go about restoration while all the time encouraging maximum use of the river by trade and pleasure.

At the time, *Pisgah* was, remarkably, still managing to trade on the navigation, her twice-weekly grain runs to Pershore forming the only regular traffic. In April, the crumbling top gates of Strensham lock gave way under the strain of years of neglect, and the river had to close completely. The newborn Trust was faced with its first emergency; the challenge of Strensham lock would determine whether its venture had any chance at all, or whether it was doomed to failure from the beginning. Desparate to obtain new gates, but without the facilities to build them themselves, representatives of the Trust approached the Docks and Inland Waterways Executive (who then had charge of almost all other inland navigations) for help. The DIWE agreed to make a new set for the Trust at its Diglis Yard, Worcester, on favourable terms (£1,103). The repairs to the lock, carried out by LANT volunteers, were successful and by the end of 1951 the lock was back in use, having received new gates and also repairs to its cill. The river was again open to Pershore, and most importantly of all, the Trust had proved themselves capable stewards of the navigation.

Some time after the river was repaired, *Pisgah* returned to trade for a further

The last diamond-shaped lock on use on the Avon, at Wyre. *Author*

Rowing boats for hire, and a typical passenger launch, upstream of the tramway bridge, Stratford upon Avon, 1992. *Author*

decade. Since then this remarkable barge, built in 1929 in Holland but used mainly in England, has been re-fitted for passenger service in France. After working as a charter boat on the Canal Lateral, *Pisgah* recently braved the Bay of Biscay to reach the newly restored River Charente, on which she continues to cruise as a hotel boat.

With the success of Strensham lock behind them, the LANT enjoyed a surge in its membership. By the close of 1951, there were 450 paid up members, who had raised over £4,000, and the Trust had purchased the navigation from Barwell (thus repaying what was in effect his loan). Consolidation of the already-navigable parts of the river took priority over extension, and members set about their task with commendable efficiency. The entrance lock to the navigation, Avon lock in Tewkesbury, was worsening quickly, and required repairs to its cills and chamber. This was carried out largely by LANT volunteers, cost £2,860, and was completed by 1952. Strensham lock, the next upstream, was further improved by the rebuilding of a derelict cottage for use by the lock-keeper. The lock at Nafford, a few miles upstream from Strensham, remained in urgent need of attention, and work there began in July 1951. Barwell surveyed the underwater parts of the structure in his own diving gear, and laid small explosive charges in the approach channels to clear them of silt. The gates were repaired, the paddle gear renewed, and a new landing stage was constructed to improve access for downstream craft.

While work was continuing on the navigable lower reaches, the Trust also turned its attention to the problems that would have to be faced in restoration of the ruined section between Pershore and Evesham. Sir Reginald Kerr made a detailed survey, and found that in places the river was too shallow to permit the use of a small outboard motor, while the lock channels and basins were badly silted. Fladbury lock was in a particularly unstable state and Walter Barrow, the owner of Cropthorne Mill (next to Fladbury lock) donated £500 to the LANT so that they could make it secure against a breach. This they quickly achieved, with money to spare.

The largest project on the unnavigable section was the rebuilding of Chadbury lock and weir, which had been utterly destroyed. The derelict site contained remains of a diamond-shaped chamber, which the LANT intended to restore. Under the guidance of David Burlingham, Chairman of the lock comittee, and Stanley Goodall, who supervised much of the work and proved expert at negotiating access to many lock sites, volunteers built steel coffer dams across the end of the access channels, and used draglines and pumps to clear out the chamber. What they found beneath the mud was in far worse condition than expected, the crumbling masonry being beyond any reasonable hope of repair. The only course of action was to build a completely lock from modern materials, a task that was obviously beyond the resources of the small Trust.

A unique solution to the problem was arrived at: the project was used as an exercise for the Royal Engineers, being the first colaboration of its kind. The arrangement was to prove highly successful from both points of view, costing the LANT only £4,000 with donations from Evesham Council, and providing a useful exercise for 50 officers and men of the Royal Engineers under the command of Lt Col G.O.N. Thompson. With money being raised by volunteers

The new LANT lock house at Evesham, built over an old sluice chamber.

of the 'Save the Avon' campaign of the LANT, work on the Chadbury site could begin in 1952. By the end of 1953, 365 tons of gravel, 275 tons of sand, 100 tons of cement and 20 tons of steel had been transformed into the newest lock in the Avon valley. Ceremonially opened by the Principal of Birmingham University, Chadbury's new lock could not be used at once, because no boats could yet reach that far upstream, but its very presence was a symbolic promise of the river's complete restoration.

In the same year (1952), the LANT published a brochure with maps, entitled *Cruising on Shakespeare's Avon*, designed to increase traffic on the navigable lower reaches. Aimed at both owners and hirers of craft, the brochure explained the work of the Trust, as well as giving information about the river. One section makes especially interesting reading, particularly after recent decades of rampant inflation. As an encouragement to would-be donors of money to the LANT, the author quoted typical costs of restoration materials. These were 10s. 6d. for 2 cwt cement, 1 guinea for 50 bricks, £5 for a set of sluice gear and £500 for a pair of lock gates!

Upstream of Nafford, the next hazard to navigation of the river was Pensham water-gate. Rather than rebuilding it, the LANT decided to dispense with it altogether (on grounds of both cost and inconvenience of use). Accordingly, it was demolished in 1956, the river bed upstream being dredged to allow the passage of boats over the shallows of the ancient ford. The river bed under Pershore bridge, just upstream of Pensham water-gate, was dredged to 5 feet and a reinforced concrete invert was inserted to support the old stone bridge, work being done by Concrete Piling Ltd of London. The excavations under the bridge uncovered a large stone cross, now safely installed in Evesham's Almonry museum.

The shallowness of the diamond-shaped Pershore lock had, for years, been a problem to helmsmen of deep-draughted vessels which were apt to run aground there. Now, with Pensham weir gone, the river was lower still. In 1954 soil tests were carried out to prepare for the lock's rebuilding as a deeper, rectangular structure. The work on the lock was completed in 1956 at a cost of £2,754. In 1954 the restoration of the very dilapidated Wyre lock began, the original diamond shape being retained. The rebuilding of the lock and dredging of its approach, by volunteers and by the contractors Thomas Vales & Sons, cost a total of £3,530. The lock was re-opened in mid-1956.

By 1957 the river was in good condition from the Severn to the tail of Cropthorne water-gate, now the only one left not only on this river, but in the whole of England. In his *Inland Waterways of England*, Tom Rolt wrote of his hope that it would be maintained in working order for many years. Unfortunately, its future became less secure once the river was being made navigable again, and the Trust decided to demolish it and to dredge a deep channel as far as Fladbury lock. The demolition of such an important relic seems an extraordinary thing for a Trust to do, and requires some explanation. As was mentioned in Chapter Two, water-gates are very slow to operate and are also dangerous (witness the accident recounted in the previous chapter). From a navigator's point of view they are a nuisance, and the dredging of the river to Fladbury would obviate the need for the gate. It was also cheaper for the Trust to demolish and dredge rather than rebuild. However, had the water-gate been preserved *and* the river dredged, both historians and navigators would have been happy, and the gate would have been retained but would not have been used. With the pressure of scant resources, the Trust did not consider this practical, and the last water-gate in England was destroyed - never again would a boat hook its bowline over Sandys' Post to wait for the water to fall. All that now remains is a little masonry and a line of rock in the river bed (*see Appendix One*).

Fladbury lock, a short way upstream from Cropthorne water-gate, was in extremely poor condition and could not be re-opened without major expenditure. Help was to arrive in the shape of Captain Vivien Bulkeley-Johnson, an enthusiastic supporter of inland navigation (he was Honorary Treasurer of the IWA) who also happened to be a senior member of Rothschild's Merchant Bank. He spent much time cruising the waterways in his narrow-boat *Willow Wren*, and when he came to Tewkesbury Robert Aickman (Chairman of IWA) introduced him to Douglas Barwell. Bulkeley-Johnson was evidently impressed by what he heard and saw of the Lower Avon - the 'Mrs Smith Trust', a charity run by his wife, made a series of donations totalling some £4,500, allowing the restoration of Fladbury Lock to proceed. Bulkeley-Johnson maintained his interest in waterways, later starting a new canal carrying company named after his own boat, just when traditional carriers were giving up in the face of road competition. The company name 'Willow Wren' survives to this day, though it is inevitably oriented more to leisure than freight).

With the demolition of Cropthorne water-gate, and the repair of Fladbury lock, the way was at last open to Evesham. The official opening took place over the Whitsun weekend, 9th June, 1962. An armada of small boats travelled from Tewkesbury to Pershore, and their crews attended a service of thanksgiving in the Abbey there. On the next day, official guests joined the flotilla as it headed upstream to Evesham, to be greeted with a Civic Reception. In his own private celebration, Douglas Barwell undertook a voyage from Evesham, down the Avon, down the Severn, and across the Irish Sea. Through its Herculean efforts, the LANT had succeeded in raising £43,000, £6,000 of which had come from the 'Mrs Smith Trust', and at least 250 volunteers had been available for work. Two years later Evesham lock was itself repaired to allow access to the lowest reach of the defunct Upper Avon- the practical limit of navigation being at Offenham. With the river fully open, the resources of the LANT could go into the improvement of its works, building of a lockhouse, moorings and sanitary points, and development of pleasure traffic. Little seems to have been done to attract any commercial carriers (the grain boats which still traded to Healing's Mill, Tewkesbury, did not even use the first Avon lock, so paid no tolls). In these days of the motorway and the articulated lorry, there is little hope of regular freight returning.

When the river was reopened, it was still operating under the 1751 rules. The navigation was a 'Free River' with its traffic barely regulated. Revenue could be raised for lock tolls, but if any vessel confined itself to reaches between locks it paid nothing, and a surprisingly large number of boat owners on the river declined to contribute to the LANT in any way. Even more worrying than lost revenue was the fact that no speed limit existed, so that a few reckless individuals were apt to ruin the peace and safety of the Avon by tearing along at ridiculous speeds, ripping off the soft banks. In 1969, Barwell told the reporter of a local newspaper that he intended to use the 1968 Transport Act to gain better control over the waterway, complaining that it was necessary to stop irresponsible boaters who did 'a hell of a lot of damage, if only to our nerves when they come flying around corners'. The changes were passed, and a new era began. The ancient system of collection of lock tolls was abolished, and instead all craft had to pay an annual (or weekly) licence fee, and comply with the 40 byelaws of the Navigation.

The next few years were to be ones of consolidation for the Lower Avon. Locks and weirs were improved and strengthened, and new facilities such as landing stages and sewage pump-out sites were installed. The tourist traffic grew, and the benefits of the reopening of the navigation therefore spread beyond the boating community.

Much credit for the success of the LANT could be attributed to the hard work and leadership of Barwell himself. His style of management was ideal for the task; he would take care to ask for the advice of his colleagues, but would not allow responsibility for action to devolve amongst members of the committee to the point where it would have been too diluted to be effective. David Cottrell, owner of Tewkesbury Marina and himself a long-serving member of the LANT committee, recalled,

> Most of us had come out of the forces and we were used to discipline, so we said what we thought about something, then kept our mouths shut as the 'colonel' made the decision.

In 1970, the New Year's Honours List announced that C.D. Barwell was to be given the Order of the British Empire. He died in the autumn of 1990.

The great success of the restoration had repercussions far beyond the river valley. Here was proof of the ability of a small group of amateurs to restore a piece of their heritage. Here was evidence of their ability to run economically a concern which had been losing money for decades. Following the Avon work, the era of canal restoration began (initially with the work of the Coventry Canal Society). In the 40 years since the beginning of the Avon's restoration, hundreds of miles of canal and river have been or are being restored by volunteers, and the decaying water-highways of England have enjoyed a resurrection in the age of leisure. Since the war, many thousands of people have sucessfully been restoring other parts of Britain's historical heritage, most obviously railways, in defiance of blinkered economic views which caused their closure and destruction. Their activity has now spread to continental Europe and North America. The inspiration and hope of restoration groups the world over owes more than a little to the dedicated pioneers of the Lower Avon.

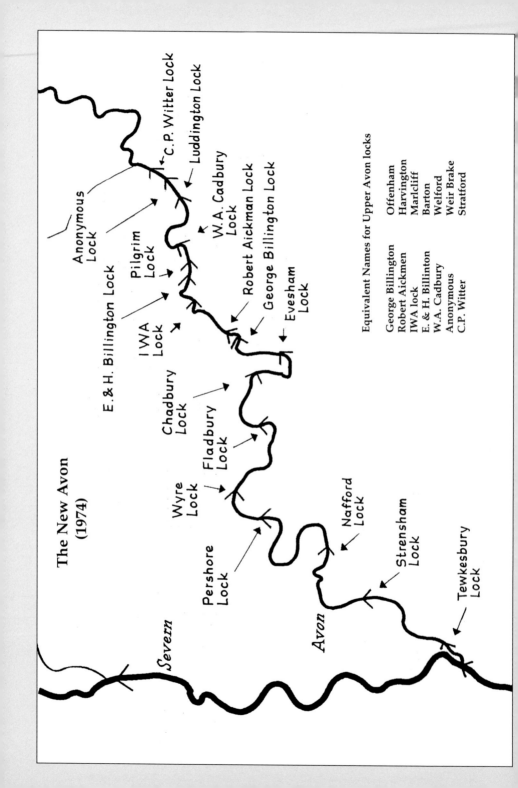

The New Avon
(1974)

Severn

C. P. Witter Lock
Luddington Lock
Anonymous Lock
E. & H. Billington Lock
Pilgrim Lock
IWA Lock
W. A. Cadbury Lock
Robert Aickman Lock
George Billington Lock
Evesham Lock
Chadbury Lock
Fladbury Lock
Wyre Lock
Pershore Lock
Nafford Lock
Strensham Lock
Tewkesbury Lock
Avon

Equivalent Names for Upper Avon locks

George Billington   Offenham
Robert Aickmen   Harvington
IWA lock   Marlcliff
E. & H. Billinton   Barton
W.A. Cadbury   Welford
Anonymous   Weir Brake
C.P. Witter   Stratford

Chapter Thirteen

The Upper Avon - Building a New Navigation

While the Upper Avon lay dormant, Stratford's other waterway slipped into terminal decline. Under the management of the Great Western Railway, the Stratford Canal carried progressively less traffic, the town receiving its last water-borne freight in the late 1920s. The northern section between King's Norton and Lapworth struggled on for a few more decades until the Great Western placed a heavy bridge across it at towpath level, blocking navigation completely. The bridge, an unremarkable type seen all over the railway system, prompted an extraordinary response by waterway enthusiasts that lead firstly to the restoration of the canal, then the river, and may one day result in completion of the navigation to Warwick.

The deliberate blocking of the King's Norton end of the canal by the GWR was in flagrant breach of a Right of Navigation, and in 1947 the Inland Waterways Association managed to have it questioned in the House of Lords. As a result, they were given the assurance that the heavy steel bridge would be lifted for any vessel requiring passage. First Tom Rolt, then Peter Scott, then other members of the IWA demanded passage for their craft, and soon the inconvenience of repeatedly sending men and lifting gear to the bridge proved greater than that of installing a movable deck. By the end of 1950, a new swing bridge was installed, and the first battle for the Stratford Canal had been won.

As use of the northern parts of the canal increased, interest grew in the derelict length between Lapworth and Stratford-upon-Avon. In 1953, the Midlands branch of the Inland Waterways Associaton published a report on the state of this section, though nothing was done until 1956, when it was rumoured that Warwickshire County Council wanted to rebuild Featherbed Lane bridge at Wilmcote without leaving navigable headroom. At once, the IWA appealed for local members to form a Protection Committee. Amongst its first members was R.D.E. (David) Hutchings, an IWA member who had already acquired a reputation for dramatic action in defence of Midlands canals, and who was destined to be a major figure in the Avon's story. The committee, which later amalgamated with a local canal club to form the Stratford-on-Avon Canal Society, set itself the goal of 'restoration of the canal to full navigable order from the Worcester and Birmingham Canal to the River Avon'. In February of the following year, two committee members hired a canoe and paid a toll to allow them to pass up and down the canal, carrying their little vessel around the ruined locks. The toll receipt was to become 'the most important piece of paper in modern waterways history'.

In 1958, Warwickshire County Council, supported by Stratford Borough Council, applied for a warrant to abandon the canal. They intended to lower bridges, to demolish the canal's great aqueduct, and to culvert the canal through Stratford itself, using its line for landfill. Under the 1888 Railway and Canal Traffic Act, the abandonment could take place only if the canal had been disused for at least three years. Using its canoe toll ticket as proof that the canal

David Hutchings preparing explosive charges near Luddington.
David Hutchings/UANT Archive

Deepening the channel below Bidford Bridge.
David Hutchings/UANT Archive

had remained at least nominally open, the Canal Society lodged an eventually successful objection to abandonment with the Minister of Transport, and tried to arrange a better future for the canal.

The result of the society's enthusiastic campaign was that the British Transport Commission, then owners of the canal, agreed to transfer it to the National Trust while the Stratford-on-Avon Canal Society performed actual restoration. Towpath clearance began in 1958, while negotiations between the National Trust and BTC were still underway, and after the formal take-over in 1960, restoration began in earnest. It was clear that such an ambitious restoration project would require a full-time manager, and David Hutchings was approached for the task. Although he was already an established architect, he agreed to suspend his career and, at the age of 33, take on the restoration of the canal provided that he was paid at a rate comparable to National Trust salary scales. Living with his wife Joan on their narrowboat *Ftatateeta*, he directed the restoration by two lengthsmen and a small army of volunteers, prisoners and Borstal boys.

The details of the restoration have been recounted in detail elsewhere; triumphing over problems posed by engineering, weather, finance, bureaucracy and frequent opposition from Stratford Council and other bodies who, in David Hutchings words, 'thought they'd break our hearts and backs over the Stratford', the voluntary navvies succeeded in achieving their aims in three years of extraordinary effort. They dredged pounds, rebuilt lock chambers, repaired and manufactured lock gates, cleared towpaths, dug out by-washes, and occasionally rode an enormous harrow towed across the channel to clear it of rubbish.

In 1964, the same year that the Lower Avon was opened to Offenham, J.D. Tompkins made the first passage down the restored Stratford Canal from Kingswood Junction to Bancroft Basin in mv *Laughing Water II*. The boat, which had once belonged to Lady Aster, was by now rather rotten and the thin layer of ice in Bacroft Basin cut through her soft timbers with the result that she sank only a few yards after leaving the basin for the waters of the Avon! The onlookers celebrated anyway, and the boat has since been restored to her former glory and is a familiar sight on the Bridgewater Canal.

Recalling the efforts and dedication of those who had worked so hard to rebuild the canal, Hutchings said,

> Those who were to do the job had nothing and knew nothing but they began with one overwhelming advantage, they were not Experts and therefore did not know what could not be done.

His personal achievement was recognized in the new year's honours list; he was appointed a Member of the Order of the British Empire.

With both the Lower Avon and the Stratford Canal now restored, the Upper Avon could be reached from both ends, but could not itself be navigated. As the neighbouring restoration schemes had progressed, interest grew in the prospect of a restored Upper Avon, which would complete a 109 mile cruising ring consisting of the Avon, Stratford Canal, Worcester and Birmingham Canal

Barton (Elsie & Hiriam Billinton lock) under construction in 1970; the view is downstream, the end of the weir being visible on the right. The elegant simplicity of the construction method is apparent.

Borstal boys building Elsie & Hiriam Billinton lock.
David Hutchings/IJANT Archive

and Severn, and would reunite Stratford with the sea.

The last serious attempt to reopen the river had been promoted 60 years earlier by the RAIA, lead by William Smith (*see Chapter Ten*). His grandson, Kenneth Gill Smith, maintained his family's interest in the Avon and supported Barwell strongly. While the LANT struggled to repair their crumbling waterway, Smith looked forward to its extension beyond Evesham and conducted exhaustive research into the ownership of the Upper Avon's title. When the National Trust took over the Stratford Canal, they made clear that they would take no responsibility for the river that their canal once owned, so the question was not simple. It is possible that British Rail was still responsible, but Gill Smith came to the conclusion that no-one still alive posessed the title, and that anyone could therefore make a claim to the river under the provisions of the 1888 Canal Traffic Act. An obvious candidate was the LANT, but Barwell estimated that the Upper Avon would cost £300,000 to restore, and would not commit the Trust to making a claim on its title. He also declined personally to manage a restoration plan carried out by any other body, although he was in no way opposed to the idea of a reopened river.

The Chairman of the Inland Waterways Association, Robert Aickman, took a strong interest in Smith's findings and the project began to be discussed very seriously. Perhaps as a result of his Grandfather's experiences, Kenneth Gill Smith realised that riparian owners would field powerful opposition to a reopened river, and insisted that a full time manager would be needed to cope with the difficulties created by them. He was supported in his opinion by a wealthy boat-owner, who had been underwriting Aickman's salary since 1961, and who approached him with a further offer in 1963; he would donate up to £90,000 to the restoration of the Upper Avon provided two conditions were met. The first was that the donation would be no more than a third of the total cost. The second was that David Hutchings should be Project Manager.

The successful completion of the Stratford Canal provided an obvious model for the Avon, so it was perhaps natural that Robert Aickman should make a tentative approach to the National Trust, via John Smith (Chairman of their general purposes committee). They were not interested in running the project so the IWA set up its own Upper Avon committee. Its first Chairman was Christopher Clifford JP, an IWA Council member who had also been Chairman of the Stratford Canal Society. Unfortunately perhaps, he held its meetings in Upton-on-Severn, which was too far from Stratford for the busy Hutchings to attend. This proved to be an obstacle, and the first year of the committee achieved rather little.

Towards the end of 1964, Aickman became aware that the benefactor was becoming disgruntled at the lack of progress and was hinting that the offer would not be extended indefinitely. He also discovered that Hutchings, who was now teaching at Birmingham University School of Architecture, was seeking a permanent position away from the waterways. He acted at once, rushing down to Stratford and, with the tact for which he was already infamous, asked Sir Fordham Flower to take over as Chairman of the Upper Avon Committee. Clifford was most unhappy about this summary imposition of Aickman's will, and resigned from the IWA Council in response. Shortly afterwards, Hutchings provisionally accepted the post of restoration manager, setting two conditions; that he should not suffer financially, and that he should have unlimited powers of day-to-day control in order that certain operational problems with the canal restoration would not be repeated - 'Either I get *carte blanche*, or I get the boot!' Both conditions were accepted. In 1965, the committee gained Trust status, David Hutchings accepted his permanent appointment starting in 1969, and the real work began.

The task of the UANT was quite different from that of either the LANT or the canal society, not only because the works of the river were in ruins. The Lower Avon had never been closed, whereas the Upper was closed in effect, at least in the sense of the 1877 court hearing (though it was still a 'free river' under the 18th century Act). This meant that the Trust had not merely to restore a navigation, but to build an entirely new one, which would not necessarily have the same features as the old.

Kenneth Gill Smith's intuition about riparian owners proved well-founded; as they had been in Sandys' time, and as they still are in present day schemes, owners of riverside land were suspicious of boats. Many, it has to be said, were very enthusiastic, and offered a great deal of help to the Trust, often giving away their land quite freely; the present condition of the river owes much to their generosity. Others were at least tolerant for the sake of the pleasure it would bring to others. A few opposed re-opening vigorously. Their grounds varied, but invasion of their privacy and increased flooding of their land were the usual reasons given. In Sandys' age, most troublemakers were dealt with rather easily, being threatened with, or actually sent to, gaol (*see Chapter One*). By the 1960s, summary imprisonment had been replaced by the need for long hours of negotiation, most of which was carried out by Hutchings personally.

The levels of water in the river were by now under the absolute control of the Severn River Authority, who had great expertise in the field of flood control. They were already considering altering the river to enable it to carry a greater volume of water, especially by removing the last remains of Cleeve weir so that the little river Arrow (which joins the Avon just upstream of it) could bring vastly increased volumes of treated sewage from new towns such as Redditch. The UANT had to plan accordingly, and even acknowledged the importance of drainage in its declared aim, 'To reopen the navigation . . . at the same time improving the drainage of the valley and also reducing the tendency of the river to flood. Following detailed consultation with the river authority, the Trust designed a new navigation featuring water levels generally below the originals. Ancient locks would be by-passed, old weirs demolished, new ones built, and a new channel would be created by extensive dredging. In some places, the level of the new water surface would be below the bed of the old navigation. Describing the sacrifices the UANT had to make, Hutchings reflected 'What we have produced is a first class land drain, which wasn't the idea at all!' The Severn River Authority gave their approval, in principle at least.

With the publication of the plans, objectors became more vociferous, and riparian owners used the local press to make known their worries that the scheme would greatly increase flooding. The River Authority responded by insisting that work on the locks could be performed only after dredging was done, but the opponents were still not satisfied. Soon, antagonism became more organised, and the County Landowners Association began to field strong opposition while the National Farmers' Union, a powerful body in an area where agriculture is one of the prime industries, shifted its position from neutrality to outright opposition.

In January 1969, at the height of the acrimony, Kenneth Gill Smith used his position as Editor of the *Evesham Journal* to publish a strong piece in support of the restoration. In it, he discussed the objectors:

> Do these dissidents wish to wreck the whole scheme and, purely from selfish motives, to prevent altogether the restoration of the Navigation? If this is the case they are acting anti-socially, irresponsibly and, to a certain extent at least, hypocritically; for they must well know that the Severn River Authority would never have given approval in principle to a scheme likely to have a deleterious effect on agriculture . . . a body such as the NFU would patently put itself in the wrong if it adopted such an attitude.

The NFU stated that they were unhappy because the Trust's proposals for controlling boats on the river were 'extremely obscure'. This point was not without foundation, but the UANT had already declared its intention to formulate by-laws. The writer went on to suggest that the UANT may improve its own public relations:

> But I think that the Upper Avon Navigation Trust could do something to improve the situation too. Apart from Mr David Hutchings, under whose direction the work is being carried out, very few people know of whom the body consists . . .

Council and parish meetings were held to discuss the alarming prospects of the new navigation, as outlined by the riparian owners. As well as flooding, the spectre of proliferating cafés and boat clubs worried villagers who feared that their peace would be shattered.

As these meetings went on, so the restoration work itself began. Hutchings explained:

> My philosophy on this river, as on the Stratford Canal, was to get it open as quickly as possible to minimal but safe standards, and then, with the money being earned work back, continually improving and developing . . .

To achieve this aim, the project was split into three parts. Phase one was restoration between Evesham and Bidford, phase two between Bidford and Binton (near Welford), and phase three between there and Stratford upon Avon. The three phases were to be tackled in numerical order. As on the canal, labour would be provided by a mixture of volunteers, prisoners and the army, under the overall control of Hutchings and the on-site supervision of Eric Prichard of Alcester Welding Services, an ex-fighter pilot who had become a very skilled welder and craftsman. The crane driver, Frank Lee, operated cranes and draglines.

Because the project involved construction of completely new locks rather than reconstruction of old ones, modern designs and materials were used throughout. All of the chambers were designed to take boats of at least 70 ft, so

The UANT's usual method of lock-construction using steel piles, shown here at Elsie & Hiriam Billinton Lock, the first on the upper river. *David Hutchings/UANT Archive*

The UANT's tug *Tom*, with two mud-barges, in the old lock cut at Harvington. *Author*

that full-length narrow-boats would be able to use the navigation for the first time. Lock bottoms were made out of concrete, and the sides of interlocking steel plates normally used for piling bridge supports etc. This method of construction made both building and maintaining the locks quick and cheap (about £5,000 each, compared with about £300,000 for a modern Thames lock), and required almost no skill from most of the workforce. It was also fairly fool-proof, which was vitally important for the Trust, who felt that if they suffered one dangerous failure their work would be shut down.

To save further time and money, second hand lock gates were used. Some were given by the Thames Conservancy, while other came from the closed Runcorn flight, that used to connect the Duke of Bridgewater's canal to the Mersey, and were rescued with the help of volunteers from Walton Gaol, Liverpool. The Manchester Ship Canal Company had obtained permission to demolish the locks, and were so keen to do so that they began work at midnight, telling the UANT that they could take whatever they could salvage but that demolition would not be delayed on their behalf. In the event, 19 lock gates were saved, some of them actually being dragged out from the flames of other burning timber in an operation that Hutchings described as being 'like going into Hades'; some of the gates still bore their scorch marks when installed on the Avon. (Ironically, the inadequacy of the campaign to keep the Runcorn flight open was one of the factors that prompted Robert Aickman to give up an active rôle in the IWA in 1964, though he continued to work hard for the Avon.)

The first old lock to be rebuilt was that at Harvington Mill, which used to be Harvington upper lock and dated from Yarranton's navigation. Work started in May 1969, when a contingent from the Army Volunteer Reserve Regiment of Belfast prepared the site for the team of 400 men (many from the 74th Engineer Regiment, Belfast), who would begin the actual construction. The remains of the old lock created severe problems for the engineers. The ruins of the original 70 ft circular chamber spoke well for the skills of its long dead builders, in that it proved strong enough to resist all attempts at driving piles through its foundations. Eventually, explosives had to be used to clear a way, the work being made even more difficult by flooding. The lock was finally completed in July 1969, though it was destined to be abandoned again not many years later.

The 'Fish and Anchor' ford, built just upstream of the site of Harvington lower lock by the council at the same time that they were supporting the original RAIA's restoration plans (*see Chapter Ten*), was still a serious obstacle to traffic. Rather than re-instating Harvington Lower Lock and making a bridge at the ford, the Trust elected to scrap the old weir and build a new lock beside the causeway, the latter forming a navigation weir in its own right. The new Offenham lock was built at some distance from the river, in order to leave room for the Severn River Authority to widen the latter for drainage purposes in the future, so it needed its own short length of canal. In addition to building the lock and canal, the Trust had to provide a bridge over its new cut to maintain access to the ford, and K. Gill Smith made a very generous donation towards the cost. In recognition, the UANT named it after his grandfather. Before the canal could be dug, two water mains had to be lowered to go underneath it. For this difficult piece of work, the UANT hired an outside contractor. As a result, the

The chamber of the now dis-used Harvington lock reopened by the UANT 20 years ago. By-passed by the Robert Aickman New lock, this one is being converted into a dry-dock.   *Author*

The memorial to the late Robert Aickman, at the lock which bears his name.   *Author*

cost of this lowering of pipes was greater than that of building the lock itself! Work on the canal and lock began, using the labour of prisoners, soldiers and volunteers, in the autumn of 1969. Their completion is associated intimately with the last days of George Billington, who had attended a talk about the UANT, given by David Hutchings, and had become very interested in its cause. Only a short while later, he learned that he was suffering from terminal cancer and had only a few weeks to live. He made a large (£3,000) donation to the Trust, and lived just long enough to see pictures of the lock and to meet those who built it in the record time of six weeks. The lock, his memorial, now bears the name 'George Billington Lock' on a large notice beside its chamber.

As the work continued, confidence in the scheme grew, and on the first of January 1970, the UANT declared that phase one of the scheme would be open by the summer of that year. By the end of 1969, the Trust had already dredged over 20,000 cubic yards of spoil from the river channel. This achievement was to prove very useful for public relations, for in spite of the very heavy rainfall of the beginning of 1970, flooding of the river was far less bad than expected. David Hutchings was very quick to point out that this was almost certainly because the building of the Navigation eased, rather than worsened, the flooding problem!

At the end of January 1970, Robert Aickman was elected Chaiman of the Trust, and took over from J.D. Tompkins (who had in turn replaced Sir Fordham Flower). The indefatigable David Hutchings continued to be project manager. Interviewed at about this time by the *Evesham Journal*, he said that his system of using prisoner labour worked very well except for the fact that the prisoners changed round too quickly for any to build up experience. On the other hand, some of them were able to advise the Army on economical use of explosives! An ex-army officer, Hutchings' took a no-nonsense attitude to his workforce of volunteers - if people did not take the work seriously, he dismissed them from the site, and later recalled, 'If I did not send them home on their knees I had wasted their time, and they performed miracles - or so 'tis said'.

His team management techniques were unusual, but effective; 'I have a theory that the smaller the gang, the more efficient each man is. Certainly if a job is going slowly, I take men away - I don't put them in - and the people that are still working take the hint and get their fingers out'.

After Harvington locks, the next great obstacle facing the navvies of the trust was the river bed at Marlcliff. Here the water levels were to be much lower than they had been in the original Navigation, and a new channel had to be dug through the river bed. As its name suggests, Marcliff is made from marl, one of the hardest clays known, and one quite unresponsive to draglines and dredgers. Its properties are like 'diamond hard rubber'. A special granite digging machine was brought down from Aberdeen, but this proved useless. The Army tried using explosives designed to blow 30-foot holes on coral reefs, but the charges simply bounced off and flew upwards, making only small depressions in the river bed. Even at the lock, trenches had to be dug for piles because they could not be driven in the conventional way. The Trust applied for permission to raise the height of the planned Marlcliff weir so that less dredging would have to be done. The water level was still lower than that of the original navigation, but of course the possibility of a higher weir re-opened the whole debate about flooding. Permission was granted by the Severn River Authority (SRA), who finally accepted that hacking through 300 yards of marl would be an impossible task, and that no risk of flooding would follow.

The assurances of the SRA were not enough to comfort Stratford Rural District Council, however, who prompted their MP to ask a question about the decision in the House of Commons. In spite of the assurances of the river authority (whose business it was to control floods), the leader of the council, John Hiatt, is quoted in the *Evesham Journal* (9th July, 1970) as saying that the raised levels would cause 'the worst flooding we have ever known' in both the Avon and Stour valleys. He went on:

> The Severn River Authority, which we considered was put there to stop flooding, will be responsible for creating worse flooding in the future than we have ever had. There is no doubt about this.

In response to this outburst, many letters were published in the local press, defending both the SRA and the UANT. One of the most interesting came from W.H. Holland, who ran a Bidford pleasure boat business which used to carry passengers to Cleeve lock. He pointed out that when, years ago, Cleeve weir was swept away, people thought that flooding would be greatly relieved. It was no better however, and Mr Holland went on to suggest that shallow water only encourages weed growth, and consequent silting up, preventing water flow.

In the end, the UANT won their case, and by the summer three new locks stood between Evesham and Bidford, at Offenham, Harvington and Marlcliff. The last named caused its builders further problems due to the marl, and explosives had to be used to make foundations. Many thousands of tons of spoil had been dredged out of the river, and along with this the dragline had uncovered the remains of an old lock gate from the last rebuilds on the Upper Avon in the preceding century. It is now in the boat museum at Ellesmere Port.

On 30th June, 1970, the first boat travelled upstream to Bidford. On board was David Hutchings, who enjoyed the voyage but admitted that they had had 'some difficulty'. During the Easter holidays of the next year, more than 30 vessels made a similar journey.

With phase one of the restoration complete, phase two could begin. Bidford bridge, an ancient structure that replaced the still more ancient Roman ford on Icknield street, was the first obstacle. With the water-gate that used to be downstream of it now gone, its foundations were too near the surface to allow navigation. Convincing the local Council that the UANT volunteers, prisoners and Borstal boys could achieve this work properly had not been easy for Hutchings, and the final position was a compromise in which the Trust had to submit monthly reports to the council. On the sixth *day* of working, they sent their first and final report! At first the authorities were disinclined to believe that the work could have been done properly in such a short space of time, but after a detailed inspection they pronounced themselves perfectly satisfied.

The river bed was then dredged to the site of Pilgrim lock, a little up-river of Grange lock's ruins. The lock, paid for by the Pilgrim Trust (a local charity), was constructed in a different way to the rest of those on the new river and was based on upper Thames structures. Instead of piles, its walls are made from concrete blocks, a method designed to avoid the need for heavy machinery. The experiment was successful and the lock was completed in six weeks despite three severe floods. The weir itself was ready at the end of 1971. In April of that year, further dredging of the river bed and the lowering of a water main opened the river as far as Barton. Phase two was now complete.

Pilgrim weir did not compensate completely for the loss of Grange weir, and removal of the old Lower Welford weir highlighted this difference. The river bed above it was quite literally dry in places necessitating the use of heavy weights and draglines, a total of four times, to produce a navigable channel. Without the very generous help of the riparian owner the task would not have been possible.

In the summer of 1971, work began on the construction of Upper Welford and Luddington locks, both near sites used by the previous navigation. In the Autumn, work began on the lock at Stratford, the UANT feeling that establishing an obvious presence in Stratford would be politically and psychologically very useful. This was an exceptionally deep chamber, substituting effectively for the old two-lock staircase at Lucy's Mill. At first, the usual method of construction was attempted, but the poor sub-soil started to give way and one of the steel walls began to collapse. Very swift action was taken by volunteers from Gloucester Gaol, who left the site of the lock and quickly reappeared with massive timber baulks which were wedged across the chamber to stabilise it. By an unspoken agreement, nobody asked from where the timber had been obtained . . . Later, the walls were moved back with the aid of hydraulic jacks, and are now safely anchored by a giant steel frame which passes over the top of the lock - an effective, if rather ugly, solution. Horrified by the gaunt appearance of the girders, so close to Stratford's famous theatre, a lady councillor asked her fellows round the committee table, 'Have you seen Mr Hutchings' abominable erection . . . ?'. Their reaction is not recorded.

The Port of London Authority offered the UANT a set of gates from the abandoned Grand Surrey Canal, for use in Stratford lock. The offer was of course accepted, but the delivery of the gates was delayed by the PLA's sudden realization that they were an essential part of London's defences against high tides! Once other protection had been arranged for the city, the crew of the nuclear submarine *Warspite* removed them from the canal and loaded them for transport to Stratford.

Much of the work in the next few months was concerned with dredging, especially above Luddington, while the last of the locks were built. In the summer of 1972, Barton lock was completed, being paid for by Elsie and Hiram Billington, parents of George Billington. The lock is named after these generous benefactors. During the summer, *Saffrons* was the first boat to make the difficult journey up river to Luddington. A major obstacle to large boats was discarded masonry under Binton Bridges, left there by the local council when they improved them. This had to be cleared, not by the council, but by the UANT.

Pilgrim lock, showing the unique method of construction using concrete blocks rather than steel piles (*Daisy*, the cruiser rising in the lock chamber, once belonged to the author).   *Author*

'Mr Hutchings' abominable erection', C.P. Witter lock, Stratford.   *Author*

In September, *Saffrons*, and *Gay Gordon* reached above Luddington weir - now only a few miles remained.

As well as the hard physical work of dredging river beds and fitting lock gates, the members of the UANT had other labours. One was fund raising, as the project was estimated to cost £300,000 and local councils had granted astonishingly little (about 0.2 per cent of the total), considering the likely effect of the navigation on the tourist industry. A creditably large amount was raised by the Trust's navvies, who sub-contracted their services to riparian projects such as the moorings for the residents of flats in Lucy's Mill. The restoration also depended in large measure on gifts of generous individuals, who together contributed about 90 per cent of the cost. The ability of the Trust to use donated funds quickly and effectively was an important factor; the manager of the restoration recalled, 'People would come along with a cheque and say "When should I come back for my lock". I'd say "Six weeks time"'.

The voice of one benefactor may speak for many: 'If we give [our money] to our church they quarrel, if we give it to the charities they waste it, but if we give it to you we see results'.

A less obvious but vitally important line of work was the acquisition of an Act of Parliament for the new Navigation. This was passed in 1972, being,

> An Act to make provision for the conservancy of the navigation of the upper part of the river Avon in the counties of Warwick and Worcester; to confer powers on the Upper Avon Navigation Trust Ltd to regulate use of such part of the River Avon by vessels; and for other purposes.

The Act decreed that,

> All the Queen's leige people shall have free liberty at all reasonable times and for all reasonable purposes in boats, barges and other vessels suitable for use on the river to pass and repass up and down the said river and to pass through and use the locks and cuts . . . and where appropriate to pass over the rollers provided for small vessels . . . subject always to the provisions of this Act.

The Upper Avon was a Free River once more!

By 1973, only one lock remained to be built before the river could be opened - Weir Brake (which was the resited 'Stour Lock' of the original plans). This lock (but not the weir) was completed in Easter of that year by four Borstal boys and Pritchard, on land given to the Trust by Edgar and Mabel Jones, and the weirs at Pilgrim lock and Luddington lock were raised to their present heights. However, passage between Weir Brake and Luddington remained difficult due to an enormous slab in the river bed. This would have been dealt with fairly easily, but for the fact that Stratford Rural District Council (which had already fielded considerable opposition to the UAN restoration) denied access to the river for nearly a year. It was finally granted only weeks before the official opening.

Higher up the reach, where a similar problem confronted the Trust, there were similar difficulties with a landowner who would not allow access. The task of removing the obstruction was finally achieved by Royal Engineers who

A hired narrow-boat on the Upper Avon. *Author*

The unusual monument which commemorates the Upper Avon's restoration. Built of the piles from which all but one of the new locks were made, the structure bears a plaque giving brief information about the restoration, a list of major benefactors, and a map of the navigation. The Royal Shakespeare Theatre can be seen in the background. *Author*

blasted a channel from the river. The landowner threatened legal action, but in fact the Trust had a right to maintain its works from the water. Just as the new channel was completed, four barges from the Waterways Recovery Group, loaded to the gunwhales with silt, sank and blocked the new channel. This time, when asked if his land might be used to crane the boat out, the landowner gave his permission for the Trust to bring any machinery they wished onto his land, because as a retired Commander of a destroyer he was unwilling to jeopardise the Royal visit. The way was cleared on 27th April, 1974, and in subsequent years the land owner became a loyal friend of the Trust.

The 28th April, 1974 saw the first boats making the journey from Evesham to Stratford-Upon-Avon for over a century; *Eoves* and *Kingfisher* arrived after a difficult journey (dredging had still to be done in places), and a month later *Jemima* completed the 'Avon Ring' cruising route.

On 1st June, 1974, Her Majesty Queen Elizabeth the Queen Mother opened the navigation officially, visiting Stratford a decade after she had opened the canal. Amongst those attending was the Poet Laureate, Sir John Betjeman, who composed the short poem 'Inland Waterway' and read it before the crowd:

> He who by peaceful inland waterways steers
> Bestirs himself when a lock lock appears.
> Slow swing the gates; slow sinks the water down;
> This lower Stratford seems another town.
> The meadows which the youthful Shakespeare knew
> Are left behind, and, sliding into view,
> Come reaches of the Avon, mile on mile,
> Church, farm and mill and lover-leaned-on stile,
> Till where the tower of Tewkesbury soars to heaven
> Our homely Avon joins the haughty Severn.
> Sweet is the fluting of the blackbird's note,
> Sweet is the ripple from the narrow boat.
>
> Your Majesty, our friend of many years,
> Confirms a triumph now the moment nears:
> The lock you have reopened will set free
> The Heart of England to the open sea.

Narrow-boat *Jubilee* carried the Queen Mother and the leaders of the UANT from Weir Brake to Stratford, between banks packed with cheering crowds. All the hard work of volunteers, whether in committee rooms or slimy lock sites, whether architects or retired servicemen, prisoners or Borstal boys, and the great generosity of the benefactors to the Trust, had paid off at last: Stratford was reunited with the sea.

After the ceremonial voyage, the guests of honour repaired to a reception at the theatre, during which Betjeman became a little agitated. Hutchings' fiancée, Felice Pearson, ascertained that the poet had left his handbag at the lock, and passed word to one of the Army officers in attendance. He at once dispatched his troops in a fast boat, and they returned a few minutes later with the bag, which they passed up to the balcony of the theatre by tying it to the end of a long pole, simultaneously restoring Betjeman's calm and creating a new piece of Avon folklore.

The new navigation proved to be an almost instant success, opening a highly popular 100-mile cruising route usually known as the Avon Ring (over 17,000 people per year now travel the river). Experience quickly showed that the published worries about flooding were utterly without foundation; there has been no serious flood since 1968. Although the trade of existing riverside restaurants has flourished since the reopening of the Upper Avon, there has been no great expansion of developments. Outside the large towns of Evesham and Stratford, there are only two marinas, both of them small and sheltered from the view of both boaters and villagers by high tree-lined banks.

Herons continue to swoop low over the water, fish continue to swim, and the feared disfigurement by oil slicks and speeding power boats remains a figment of imagination. Indeed the depth provided by weirs and dredging, and the disturbance and aeration of the water by sluices and boats, have protected the river's ecology from fertilizer run-off and the millions of gallons of treated sewage that now flow into its waters. The Trust's project manager said recently:

There is no doubt about it, it would have been a sewer by now; the rubbish would have come down, the weed would have grown and God knows what would have happened to this section of river if it had not been restored.

Anglers have also appreciated this point. During the restoration, the huge Birmingham Anglers' Association were immensely supportive of the Trust, and contributed to its funds. In 1971, the BAA's fishery officer wrote to the Trust, 'Thank you most sincerely for the work you have carried out . . . I think you are doing a wonderful job'.

Naturally, the work did not stop with the opening but continues to this day, aided by the Trust's strategy of concentrating on navigation matters rather than spending time organising social events for members. Further dredging has been performed, and mooring sites have been built at many places along the navigation. The floor of Stratford lock has been raised (thanks to the level allowed by Weir Brake, and a donation from Colin Witter after whom the new lock is named), to the extent that its steel beams are no longer needed. Over the years, however, the town has grown to like them, and argued against their demolition; they have become a permanent feature of the riverside scene. In 1982, a new lock was opened at Harvington, to replace the first built by the Trust which was subject to severe silting and also difficult to reach with a full-length narrow-boat because of a sharp corner; it has been called the 'Robert Aickman New Lock'. The old lock, abandoned for a time, has been converted into a dry dock.

In contrast to the LANT (which has the expense of looking after very old locks and weirs), the UANT is able to support the maintenance of its modern navigation entirely from its own income, and requires no grant aid. This is a source of great pride to Hutchings in particular:

I'm awfully glad that we earn our own living actually. When I took this on we claimed that we could restore waterways more cheaply than they could be closed, and that when they were opened they would be self-supporting . . . I can see no point in producing a liability.

The great achievement of the UANT staff and volunteers in building their new river is perhaps underlined most clearly by a recent statement of the President of the Association of Pleasure Craft Operators: 'The Upper Avon is by far the pleasantest river to navigate. Other navigation authorities please copy'.

Original Upper Avon Locks		New Upper Avon Locks	
Name	*Original*	*Planned new*	*Actual*
(Lower Harvington)	4 ft 8 in.	-	-
Offenham	-	2 ft 2in.	2 ft 2 in.
Upper Harvington	4 ft 8 in.	5 ft 5 in.	5 ft 5 in.
Cleeve	4 ft 9 in.	-	-
Marlcliff	-	3 ft 9 in.	4 ft 9 in. adjustable
Bidford Flash-lock	0 ft 8 in.	-	-
Barton	-	3 ft 5 in.	5 ft 0 in.
Grange	4 ft 9 in.	-	-
New Grange	-	2 ft 5 in.	6 ft 0 in.
(Lower Welford)	2 ft 0 in.	3 ft 0 in.	- (not built)
Upper Welford	6 ft 4 in.	5 ft 5 in.	7 ft 5 in.
(Lower Luddington)	2 ft 0 in.	-	-
Upper Luddington	3 ft 0 in.	3 ft 5 in.	5 ft 5 in.
Stour	-	4 ft 0 in.	- (resited)
Weir Brake	-	-	4 ft 0 in.
Lucy's Staircase	7 ft 4 in.	-	-
Stratford	-	7 ft 5 in.	5 ft 5 in.
	46 ft 11 in.	40 ft 5 in.	40 ft 7 in.

(Names in brackets indicate locks dating from the 19th century improvements. Most of the locks have now been named after benefactors. In order, these names are; George Billington, Robert Aickman, IWA, E.H. Billington, Pilgrim, W. Cadbury, & C.P. Witter. All numerical data from *Waterways World* June 1990.)

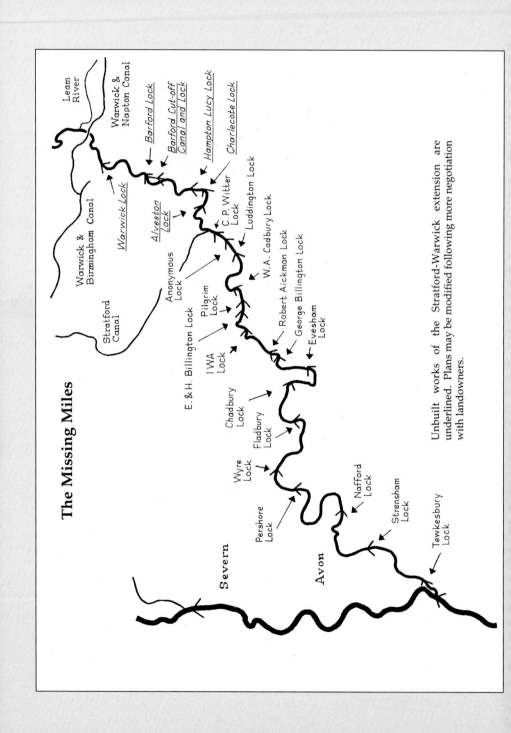

The Missing Miles

Leam River

Warwick & Birmingham Canal

Warwick & Napton Canal

Barford Lock

Barford Cut-off Canal and Lock

Hampton Lucy Lock

Charlecote Lock

Warwick Lock

Stratford Canal

Alveston Lock

C. P. Witter Lock

Luddington Lock

Anonymous Lock

Pilgrim Lock

W.A. Cadbury Lock

E. & H. Billington Lock

Robert Aickman Lock

IWA Lock

George Billington Lock

Evesham Lock

Chadbury Lock

Fladbury Lock

Wyre Lock

Nafford Lock

Severn

Pershore Lock

Strensham Lock

Avon

Tewkesbury Lock

Unbuilt works of the Stratford-Warwick extension are underlined. Plans may be modified following more negotiation with landowners.

Chapter Fourteen

The Missing Miles

The Avon Navigation was never intended to end at Stratford. The Earl of Warwick planned a navigation from Tewkesbury to his castle, William Sandys' 1635 Letters Patent extended all the way to Coventry, and the 1751 Act (24 Geo. II) made the Avon a 'free river' throughout Warwickshire, Worcestershire and Gloucestershire. In their Articles of Association, The Upper Avon Navigation Trust followed tradition by naming Guy's Cliff (upstream of Warwick) as the terminus of their restoration plans. They have not yet succeeded in carrying out any work beyond Stratford.

When the UANT's 1972 Act was being planned, it was clear to the Trust that, while it could be fairly certain of restoring navigation from Evesham to Stratford, it would face far greater opposition further upstream. It therefore concentrated initially on completing the 'Avon ring', assuming that once it had proved itself to be a trustworthy navigation authority the Warwick extension would be more welcome. Consequently, the 1972 Avon Act (Elizabeth II cap.20) confined itself to the river below Alveston Sluice, at the upper end of the Stratford pound, and the river beyond that was planned as a rather separate entity, the 'Higher Avon'. The Trust made no secret of its ultimate intentions and during the 1974 Upper Avon re-opening, HM the Queen Mother told Hutchings that she looked forward to a similar event in Warwick, though she warned him not to take 10 years this time!

In 1976, two years after the restored Upper Avon had opened, Hutchings and others formed the Higher Avon Navigation Trust, dedicated to improving the navigation to Warwick and connecting it to the Warwick and Napton Canal. Now part of the London-Birmingham Grand Union system, this canal had been widened to 14 ft gauge in the 1930s, so its connection to the Avon would have provided a new broad-beam route between the rivers Thames and Severn (the other broad cross-country routes were then in ruins). In this respect the HANT's plans recalled those of the 1919 Avon Joint Committee (*see Chapter Eleven*).

From an engineering point of view, Hutchings considered the river between Alveston and Guy's Cliff to be 'an infinitely better navigation than the Upper Avon is even now'. Much of it is deep, and long stretches are already fully navigable by large vessels, the reach between Warwick and Barford being used by a trip boat until recently. To create through navigation to Warwick, the Trust planned six locks similar to those on the Upper Avon, four to by-pass existing weirs at Alveston, Hampton Lucy, Barford and Warwick, and two to raise levels over shoals at Charlecote and Sherbourne. They also planned to dredge about 20 per cent of the river to provide adequate depth over remaining shallows. The plans were submitted to the Severn River Authority, and were approved in 1978.

A number of alternative designs were considered for connection to the Warwick and Napton (Grand Union) Canal, which crosses the Avon at

A scene typical of the Upper Avon between Alveston and Warwick - this unrestored section has some of the most beautiful scenery on the river. *Author*

Shallows at Hampton Lucy, which would be made navigable by a combination of dredging and the construction of a lock near Charlecote. *Author*

Warwick by means of an aqueduct 35 feet high. One possible route used the little river Leam, which runs very close to the canal just east of Leamington Spa, and flows into the Avon a little way upstream of the aqueduct. Making the lowest reaches of the Leam navigable with locks, and making a short cut between it and the canal, would provide an indirect connection with the Avon.

A more direct approach, and the current favourite, is the building of a single large lock of 35 ft rise at the aqueduct site. The structure that has been designed by the Trust would be situated at the site of a redundant power station next to the aqueduct. Rather than being sunk in the ground like a conventional lock, it would have walls that tower high above, and its chamber would be filled by pumped river water to conserve levels in the canal. The top end of the chamber would communicate with the canal by means of a short aqueduct, the design of which currently incorporates a narrow section to prevent broad beamed craft entering the canal (British Waterways insist on this feature, because they argue that the Grand Union canal north of Berkhampstead is not a true broad-gauge waterway although it has broad-gauge bridges, locks and tunnels; their view continues to attract controversy).

When the HANT submitted its plans for extending restoration to Warwick, they estimated that the project could be completed in two years for approximately £500,000. They have never been given a chance to start work. Looking back to the decision to limit the 1972 Act to Alveston sluice, from a perspective afforded by 20 years of frustration, Hutchings recently reflected: 'We made a tactical mistake. At that time we could have got the thing through and we would have been there by now'. Far from reducing antagonism to the Higher Avon scheme, the great success of the Evesham-Stratford section seemed to harden it. He continued: 'In England today, success is not forgiven, as you know . . . all those who opposed us on the canal and on the river got together to oppose us [on the river's extension]'.

The first really powerful expression of protest by riparian owners was made against the HANT's wish to acquire control of the navigation by means of a Private Bill. Those opposing the HANT alleged that the Avon upstream of Stratford had never been a navigation, and that a full Act of Parliament would be required to make it so. The Trust cited the 1751 Act in its favour, and in 1979 Parliament agreed with them. However, the incident had demonstrated such strong resistance to the waterway's improvement that the Bill was withdrawn temporarily. Like the UANT, the HANT wished to operate wherever possible with the consent and encouragement of riparian owners and local people.

Amongst the strongest objectors to the Higher Avon improvement, in the early days at least, was the National Trust. Although this body had been enthusiastic for other waterways, having taken over the river Wey and Stratford Canal, and having once considered taking over a large part of the narrow canal network, it was in a difficult position on the Avon. It had become the custodian of Charlecote House and Deer park, former owners of which had been obstructing navigation even at the turn of the century (*see Chapter Eleven*). The National Trust feared that the presence of boats would disturb the deer and bring trespassers to the park, especially because of the HANT's planned lock. Until they could be convinced that the Avon above Stratford was ever *used* as a

Even though the river upstream of Alveston is not navigable by large vessels, small boats such as these at Warwick are available to give their hirers a taste of the top end of the Upper River.

Author

The Avon at Warwick. *Author*

navigation, the National Trust considered the scheme to be a new development rather than a restoration, and opposed it. Madame Tussauds, owners of Warwick castle, had similar concerns about the setting of their tourist attraction.

Opposition from these two influential landowners, together with that of local farmers and Stratford Council, was clearly a major obstacle. However, the changing fortunes of the National Trust's own navigation gave the HANT cause to hope that a compromise might be reached. During the late 1970s, while the Upper Avon was being steadily improved and attention was being focussed on its extension, the condition of the National Trust's Stratford Canal deteriorated markedly. Few boats had used the re-opened waterway in the 1960s (about 300 per year), and its licence income was so low that the planned improvement to its hastily-restored engineering works fell far behind schedule. By 1970, maintenance was barely keeping pace with deterioration although more boats were passing along the canal.

The opening of the 'Avon Ring' in 1974 created a sudden surge in traffic, which brought a welcome increase in income but also a disproportionate rise in damage to the locks and towpath especially from inexperienced hirers of heavy narrow-boats. It also meant that the canal was so busy in the summer that there was never time to maintain it. The situation worsened, and by 1977 the National Trust announced its willingness to transfer the canal to another body. Three years later, it was becoming clear that there was a serious risk of it being abandoned altogether. The British Waterways Board, which was responsible for all navigations nationalised in 1948, offered to take it back as a 'remainder' waterway (a classification that would not give it a guaranteed future), but only if the National Trust paid them a substantial sum to cover the backlog of work.

Knowing that the canal's failure would deal a terrible blow to the waterways restoration movement, David Hutchings and members of the local IWA formed the Stratford Canal Advisory Committee, which became the Stratford Canal Trust. They offered to restore again a canal that he had handed over to the National Trust, in good condition, only a decade and a half before. The determination is conveyed well in Hutchings' own words:

> Heaven knows, [the 1960s restoration] cost me my marriage, it cost me my family, it cost me my career, it cost me a lot of money, so I was fairly fed up when it went to the wall . . . but we said we'd go back and do it again . . . at a much lower figure than the Board was asking for.

The Stratford Canal Trust was determined that this time the restoration of the canal would not be followed by another decline. It therefore made it a condition of the take-over that the National Trust and local authorities with an interest in the Stratford Canal should give their fullest support to the Higher Avon Scheme. The Canal Trust saw the success of river as vitally important for two reasons; it would provide an alternative route for traffic passing through Stratford, and thus relieve the canal, and it would also earn more than enough money to maintain both waterways.

Support of the Higher Avon scheme proved too much to ask, and negotiations reached a stalemate. Eventually, the National Trust accepted a

Two views of a model of a proposal for the Avon-Grand Union Link Lock.

modified offer from British Waterways Board, and the canal passed to them in 1988. It has remained open.

Following this setback, the Higher Avon's supporters reconsidered the strategy they had adopted in the 1970s. The use of a separate name for the Alveston-Guy's Cliff section of the river was a tactic that had failed. It had become irrelevant and was dropped, the campaign passing back to the Upper Avon Navigation Trust and the Higher Avon scheme now being referred to as 'completion of the Upper Avon Navigation'. The UANT was to face a long battle.

During the 1940s, 1950s and 1960s, associations that lobbied for use and restoration of waterways were seen by the general public as conservation groups, 'Green' in present-day language. They brought back clear water, tidy banks and thriving wildlife to the derelict ditches that old canals had become. The waterways they restored became peaceful havens in which walkers, anglers and boaters could rest from the strains of urban life. Only riparian owners and those with a special interest in the closure of navigations (such as road authorities with expensive bridges to maintain) tended to oppose the volunteer navvies.

From the late 1970s, this started to change and by the mid-1980s, waterways enthusiasts found their work castigated by an increasing number of vociferous protesters. The grounds for this clamour were varied, and conveyed in many ways the message that the waterways movement was becoming a victim of its own success.

Protests came from many directions. Some attacked the waterways for providing an 'alternative' environment that encouraged 'dropouts and workshy attitudes'. Others attacked reopening of inner city waterways because they did not wish their neighbourhoods to be invaded by 'yuppies'. Most, however, used the increasingly fashionable interest in green issues to attack navigation on environmental grounds. It was here that the volunteer navvies were at most risk from the fruits of their own labours. In many successful projects, they had worked for decades to restore navigation to canals that had become stagnant eyesores, and in so doing they had created exceptionally rich havens for wildlife. Their outstanding conservation work threatened to prove their downfall. On the Basingstoke Canal, for example, naturalists who had not lifted a finger towards restoration were so pleased with the wildlife they saw returning to the rebuilt waterway, that they wished the use of boats to be severely restricted or banned lest the wildlife should be disturbed. For a while, the Nature Conservancy Council lent its considerable weight to the naturalist's cause. There followed similar demands to limit boat movement on the nearly-restored Kennet and Avon Canal, and even to close parts of the main cruising network to protect water plants (although though those plants must have tolerated boats to be there in the first place!).

The 'anti-waterways movement' gained strength rapidly, especially where riparian owners were opposing restoration. Even when they were actively building nature reserves (e.g. Montgomery Canal), navigation authorities and voluntary bodies were branded a 'threat' to the countryside by a County Landowners' Association. Action against navigators was by no means confined to the letters pages of newspapers; boaters who exercised their undoubted right of navigation up the Severn to Bewdley were greeeted with 'abuse, rotten eggs and other unpleasant missiles'.

Against this background, those who objected to the Upper Avon extension to Warwick could be sure of attention, and could hope to attract support from an audience sympathetic to wildlife and already impotently angry about the environmental havoc wreaked by construction of the nearby M40 motorway. In an article in *Waterways* summarising the latest broadsides that had been fired against navigation generally, John Gagg (ex-Chairman of the IWA) wrote,

> As often, the Higher Avon bears the brunt again. The venom of the opposition is increasingly disturbing, and surely no sane reader stomachs it. But it keeps flowing, especially in the *Leamington Spa Courier*. Even the manager of [a major waterside tourist attraction] bursts forth now, all about illegal mooring, access for louts, destroying wildlife, trespass, vandalism, boat queues, litter, 'casual toilets' - good heavens, who's he talking about?

Other letters that appeared in the local press referred to the river becoming 'an aqueous race-track', while it was said that in Stratford boats were 'killing off the local swan population with the lead in their fuel'. Though patently absurd (marine diesel never has had lead additives) this last claim convinced many nature lovers, until the ban on anglers' lead shot was followed by an almost immediate restoration of the swan population!

David Hutchings dismissed such outbursts of the opposition as 'mildly hysterical'. Dr Dennis Hall a fisheries expert called in to assess the effects of the projected Higher Avon on fish stocks, was less restrained: 'The first thing I discovered was the intricate tissue of reliable information, distortions, half truths and downright lies spread by some opponents of the scheme'. He concluded that the plans for the river would have no detrimental effects.

In the face of such a strident clamour of disinformation, those fighting for navigation had to devote much energy to explanation, education and negotiation. Distancing themselves from the speed-obsessed advertisments for power boats found in sea-orientated magazines, the Avon's boaters invited those worried about their behaviour to visit the restored part of the river and judge for themselves. The UANT pointed out that it had never received a letter of complaint from a landowner about the conduct of any crew. Restoration groups, navigational authorities and the Inland Waterways Association began to broadcast the results of properly scientific studies of waterway ecology, to demonstrate the richness of wildlife in channels kept deep, aerated, and free of surface weed by the effects of navigation. The UANT also drew attention to the economic effects that followed reopening of the Avon up to Stratford, with an obvious implication for waterside communities towards Warwick.

Gradually, attitudes changed and compromises became more possible. Historical research (the results of which appear in previous chapters) has established that the right of navigation to Warwick was exercised several times in the river's history, and has also revealed that the earliest serious plans for a navigation originated in Warwick Castle itself. The Castle's current owners

The aqueduct by which the Warwick and Napton (Grand Union) canal crosses the Avon at Warwick. The site for the proposed linking lock is on the left bank just beyond the trees.   *Author*

have become interested in this connection, and Hutchings believes that they may drop their opposition to restoration provided that access to their land is controlled and the setting of the castle is not spoiled. The UANT plan to meet these wishes by building the lock channel behind an existing small island.

The National Trust has long expressed concern about access to its land and disturbance to the setting of Charlecote House. To keep boaters away from this sensitive site, Hutchings has planned a new canal and lock to be built on the far side of the river behind a screening embankment, and has been told that the National Trust will not oppose the scheme provided its neighbours are content with it.

The loop of river at Barford contains a genuinely ecologically-sensitive site; its bed supports a rare assembly of fresh water molluscs whose ecology could be affected by the presence of boats. The suggested solution is again a canal, which will run next to the village's projected road by-pass and will keep boats well away from the fragile loop. The plans are currently receiving attention from the planning authority.

With slow progress being made, and negotiations with landowners continuing, the UANT is gaining confidence again. Though Hutchings is wont to remark ruefully that he has 'spent the last 20 years *not* restoring waterways', he now talks optimistically about starting work on the Upper Avon's extension, the idea being to begin improvements wherever agreement has been reached in the hope that remaining obstacles will fall in time.* With luck, boats will be cruising to Warwick around the turn of the century.

---

* Perhaps a temporary solution would be the fitting of landing stages and punt rollers to the existing weirs, to facilitate the passage of small craft and thus allow citizens of Stratford and Warwick to enjoy their two-and-a-half-centuries-old right of navigation.

One of the Navigational Hazard Warning Signs installed by the NRA; at times of flood the lower half of the sign is hinged up to reveal a notice *advising* (only) that navigation should cease. The accompanying notice for 'River Watch' is a depressing sign of the times, and underlines the fact that boats have become tempting targets for thieves. *Author*

Present day craft on the Upper River - a hired narrow-boat passes a private sea-going sloop (temporarily devoid of its mast). The vessels are in the canal at George Billinton lock. *Author*

Chapter Fifteen

The River Today

It is now over 350 years since the Avon's waters first carried large vessels, and since that time the navigation has been in a state of constant change. The language of 'restoration' notwithstanding, the river will never again see Sandys' barges, the little Upper Severn sailing trows, *Bee* steaming ahead of her tow, or the elegant passenger launches of an age gone by. Her waters no longer carry grain to their lonely mills, and bankside towns obtain their fuel and merchandise by improved versions of the roads which the Avon once replaced. Rivers are never stagnant, and the new navigation has a rôle not as a museum-piece to remind one of days gone by, but as a vibrant part of late 20th century life.

The tremendous increase in both free time and average disposable income enjoyed by citizens of post-war Britain has nurtured a great rise in enthusiasm for boating, and most waterways survive primarily for leisure. Between 1946 and 1990, the number of hire-boat holidays taken in Britain per year increased from 80,000 to over 600,000, with the Avon becoming established as one of the more popular routes. It now has five hire-boat businesses, at Tewkesbury, Evesham, Bidford, Welford and Stratford, and plays host to many visiting craft from the Severn and the narrow canals of the Midlands. The vessels used in the new trade bear little relationship to those of the old river. Most of them are constructed completely of steel, with characteristically crude hulls based loosely on those of working narrow-boats, full-length cabins, unsheltered tiller steering, and single diesel or battery-electric engines. These are extremely popular because they offer the hirer the choice of both narrow canals and the broader river systems. Others, mostly based on the Severn, are beamy, flat-bottomed plastic boats, similar to 'Broads cruisers', and also powered by diesel.

In addition to the hire cruisers, there are also many private craft on the river. There is much more variety here, with sailing craft, small outboard-driven cabin cruisers, converted life-boats, large sea-going motor-yachts, narrow-boats and the occasional steam-launch. Moorings have been provided either in purpose-built marinas (built where planning authorities are satisfied that they will not interfere with the aesthetic appeal of the river) or along the banks of some meadows. Day-tripping boats continue to be used, especially in Stratford-upon-Avon, and punts may still be hired from quays used for that purpose a century ago. In all, the Avon carries some 10 to 20 thousand journeys per year.

From a navigator's point of view, the river has improved almost out of recognition since the days of Sandys and Yarranton. Nowadays, navigation continues even in the driest of summers, and the channel is four feet deep even in the worst of places. All of the lock chambers are long enough to take full length narrow-boats (70 feet), and the lock at Tewkesbury is power-assisted. The water-gates have gone, sadly, but so have their attendant delays. A warning system has been installed to provide early notice of flooding, and signposts have been erected to make clear the difference between lock and weir

137

New 'warehouse style' apartment block at Evesham. It is built on the site of a ballroom, which replaced a pleasure boat yard, which in turn replaced real commercial warehouses.   *Author*

Apartments at the site of Lucy's Mill, Stratford, whose owners introduced the Avon's first regular steam service.   *Author*

channels. Both trusts have endeavoured to provide as many mooring points as possible, though the fact that most riverside land is private has limited their number, causing one of the few points of dissatisfaction expressed by the river's users. From the point of view of walkers and anglers, riverside land is becoming more accessible, most notably by the recent opening of a trail along the entire length of the Upper Avon.

The trade brought by the Avon continues to benefit commerce on its banks, though it does so by methods quite different from those envisaged by Sandys. Boat builders, hire-boat companies and marina owners are most obviously profitting from it. In addition, pubs, shops and restaurants along the river benefit tremendously from passing trade; a recent independent survey revealed that the river as a whole brings approximately six million pounds per year to its valley's economy.

The changing use of the navigation is also reflected in its physical environment. As the railways and roads eclipsed the waterway as a major carrier of freight, so industry in the towns along its length began to move away from its banks. Where Evesham's warehouses once stood tall, the Workman Gardens provide a peaceful riverside picnic place for the rapidly expanding population of a town now surrounded by new housing estates, while a brand-new block of apartments has been built on the opposite bank - strangely enough in the style of a warehouse! It replaces a ball-room, which in its turn replaced a boat yard. Stratford-upon-Avon, the town concerned above all others to maintain its 'Olde Worlde' image, ironically shows the river's changing rôle most clearly. The great Lucy's Mill, pioneer of steam haulage, is now no more than a collection of residential apartments, while the reach upstream of Lucy's lock has lost almost every sign of its status as an inland port. Not only have the river-side warehouses (near Clopton Bridge) gone, but even the busy transhipment site of Bancroft Basin, where river, canal and tramway met, is now a carefully tended garden for the benefit of Stratford's profitable trade in tourists.

Much, then, has happened in the development of this river of the leisure age. Some aspects of a waterway never change, and the Avon Navigation's current owners have to take as much care of their works as did their illustrious predecessors. Lock gates need renewing, channels silt up, old weirs threaten to collapse, and money must be raised to keep everything in order. The two Trusts have evolved slightly different strategies to meet these challenges, partly because of their different present circumstances and partly for historical reasons.

The UANT has, in one sense, the easier task. It runs the only navigation in the country to be built specifically for use by pleasure craft, so all of its works are modern and are built to withstand the onslaught of even the most brainlessly-navigated hire craft. Maintenance is therefore easier than on the Lower Avon, but is by no means trivial. The UANT has remained a small body, of about 100 members with a Council of only 10, who act via a Project Manager (David Hutchings). The trust is dedicated purely to navigation, having neither social activities nor even a newsletter. Its paid staff is minimal, consisting of the project manager, his part-time secretary and two engineering assistants. Its plant includes the tug *Tom*, the barge *Cammell* (which is large enough to provide a working platform for excavators etc.), two mud barges, and essential land-based construction machinery. Through raising money from boat licences, work for external riverside owners, and some other sources of private income, the UANT is now completely self-sufficient, and is even in a position to fund initial work on its extension to Warwick.

The LANT restored an ancient river built for occasional passage of cargo boats, and in many ways less suited for novice pleasure skippers. The old walls of lock chambers have been a considerable source of trouble, while some ancient weirs have been in danger of collapse. It is a larger body than the UANT, having over 500 members who enjoy 'social' benefits as well as the navigation itself. The LANT is controlled by a 9-member executive committee drawn from a council of 18, and places day-to-day control in the hands of a 16 reach-masters rather than a single project manager. Staff include two lock-keepers and three part-time assistants, though the membership provides an additional volunteer workforce for maintenance duties. The LANT fleet of work boats include the tug *City*, powered workboat *Jubilant*, an ex-Ouse barge *Lantern*, mud hoppers *Robert Aickman* and *Douglas Barwell*, the pontoon *Gallant*, and two small tenders.

Both Trusts are profitable, which is all the more remarkable given that the nationalised waterway system is said to consume £30,000 per mile per year. Though they remain independent bodies they co-operate extensively, especially in carrying out work for the Avon Weirs Trust (AWT), a body formed in 1991 to 'ensure the long term stability of the river system'. The funding of the AWT, most of which comes from the National Rivers Authority and some of which comes from the navigation trusts, is dedicated to the upkeep of weirs for the purposes of safety, drainage, navigation, conservation and water supply. The AWT has already carried out substantial work on the old mill weirs of the Lower Avon.

Increasing co-operation between the UANT and LANT has stimulated discussions on their possible future amalgamation. So far, the initiative has been resisted, especially by certain members of the UANT, but as the draft designs of a new combined Avon Navigation Trust are altered to meet objections that have been raised, it seems more probable that amalgamation will eventually take place (though probably not for some years). This would place the whole river from Tewkesbury to Guy's Cliff in the control of a single body, for the first time in almost three centuries.

The forces which shape the Avon's history continue to evolve. While the old pressures of trade and competition have diminished, new ones arise, such as the tensions between preservation and modernisation, and between commercial development and environmental conservation. The story of a river can never really be finished. Whatever is to come, I wish all those who come to know the Avon's waters the greatest pleasure in watching their history unfold.

Appendix One

An Historical Guide to Cruising the Avon

This appendix is intended to be of use mainly to navigators who wish to view features important to the Avon's history, most of which have been mentioned in previous Chapters. Many of the sites are also accessible to land-based explorers, who will find O.S. 1/50,000 maps 150 and 151 useful.

All directions are based on a journey *down* the river, from its junction with the Stratford Canal.

Bancroft Basin, Stratford-Upon-Avon
The attractive Bancroft Basin, which is a welcome contrast from the industrial scenery of most of the Stratford Canal's route through the town, is now one of the main temporary mooring sites for visiting canal craft. Being near to the theatre, the air of the place rings to the multilingual chatter of visiting tourists come to pay homage to Shakespeare. The beautifully tended gardens bear little witness to the appearance of the place in the heyday of water transport - a busy collection of quays surrounded by warehouses and a network of sidings of the Stratford and Moreton tramway (*Chapter Seven*). Here coal, grain, wool and a host of other commodities were transhipped between narrowboat, river barge and tram-wagon. Of the two original basins, only one remains, though the old canal which connected to the basin now under the gardens remains as a short spur leading off the extant moorings. On the opposite side to the theatre there is a short length of plateway on which stands the sole surviving tram-wagon, now beautifully preserved. Keen walkers can follow the trackbed across the river bridge and on out of Stratford towards the Cotswolds until its route merges with that of the modern A34(T).

Lucy's Locks and Mill
Less than a mile downstream of Bancroft, the first lock (C.P. Witter) comes into view. The unusual construction (with the sides held back by a rectangular steel frame) replaces Lucy's locks, a two-lock staircase whose foundations are buried under the mound of earth to the left of the new structure. Across the weir was Lucy's Mill, whose voracious appetite for grain provided a living for bargemasters over the years. Indeed, the introduction of steam haulage on the navigation was due to the far-sightedness of Thomas Lucy and Son who wished to improve the efficiency of corn supply. Sadly, the mill is no more, having been replaced by a 'development' of rather expensive riverside flats - a fate all too common for old mills and warehouses on inland waterways.

SMJR Bridge
Just downstream of Lucy's Mill is a footbridge, built in 1934 on the approximate site of a bridge first built in 1599 and subsequently modified to facilitate navigation. Following the footbridge is an arched structure which once carried the Stratford and Midland Junction Railway, whose acronym SMJR was locally redefined as 'slow, mouldy and jolting railway'! Slow it may have been, but by providing a route (via Broom Junction) along the Avon valley from Stratford, via Evesham, to Ashchurch (near Tewkesbury) and eventually Gloucester, this railway provided keen competition for the Navigators. Though it was not opened until the Upper Avon was almost derelict, its presence did detract from later arguments for the improvement of the water route to Stratford.

The submerged wall of Welford Lower lock, now no more than a hazard to navigation for incautious skippers. *Author*

The old gate support at the upstream end of Welford Lower lock. This chamber, being only 60 ft long, would have been too small to admit a standard narrow-boat, forcing goods to be trans-shipped at Stratford. *Author*

Ironically, the railway itself closed during the 1960s, when the restoration of the Upper Avon was just beginning, and its old bridge is now threatened by the works of a bypass and the relentless spread of modern housing.

Weir Brake Lock

This dates from the UANT's restoration, and is close to the site of the ancient Stratford (Stour) water-gate removed during the 1820s river improvements.

GWR Bridge

A short way down the straight reach below Weir Brake is a second railway bridge, which carried a railway from Birmingham, via Stratford, to the GWR's Worcester-Oxford line at Honeybourne, and was later extended to Cheltenham. One of the last main-line railways to be built in this country, it has now closed, but its southern end, between Winchombe and Toddington, Gloucs, has been restored for use by steam locomotives, and is well worth a visit. The preserved section, currently extending between Toddington and Gretton can be reached from Evesham by bus. (Having helped to lay part of the track, the author is especially keen to see the line supported!)

The Stour

Once it has rounded the bend beyond the GWR bridge, the waters of the Avon are augmented by those of the Stour. This little river was to have been part of Yarranton's great link across England, and the land at the juction of the waters would have become the flax town of New Haarlem (*Chapter Three*). In fact, the Stour remains unnavigable to this day, and only the few houses of Milcote mark the proposed site of Yarranton's 'industrial new town'. Just below the confluence of the two rivers lies a great rocky slab, hidden from view under the waters of the river. This was one of the most serious obstacles to the 1974 re-opening of the Upper Avon (*Chapter Thirteen*).

Luddington Locks

The next old lock site is reached at Luddington, the village at which Shakespeare is said to have been married. Moorings are provided above the lock cut, and visitors can take advantage of these to disembark and view the remains of the old Upper Luddington lock. Part of its cut still survives as a basin for local craft. Beyond the end of this, and across a rough track, are situated the last remains of a 70 ft circular lock chamber, now little more than a depression in the ground. The best preserved part is probably that at the very lower end, where the great stone abutments still stand. Once, Luddington had two locks to its name, and the ruins of the lower one lie just downstream of Luddington Island, in the lea of a steep escarpment. Access to the site of the lock, built in the 1820s improvement scheme, is difficult by water, and impossible by land unless permission of landowners is obtained. What can be seen from the river is a narrow and weed-choked channel leading off the left bank to a tree-covered pool which is all that remains of the lock chamber. The presence of the weir is rather more obvious, and care must be taken to avoid its foundations.

Upper Welford Lock

The present structure dates from 1971, but next to it, on the island between it and the weir, can be found a large circular hole, extremely overgrown. This was the old Welford

The remains of Cleeve lock, now high and dry due to the lowered level of the river. The chamber shows the diamond shape characteristic of the older Avon locks, with a width of about 45 ft in the middle (and about 13 ft at the entrances). *Author*

The remains of the rectangular chamber of Lower Harvington lock, built during the 1830s improvements to the river. The curved masonry that once supported the lower lock gates can be seen just inside the entrance. *Author*

Upper lock, raising boats over the weir powering the mill, whose buildings now constitute elegant country homes.

Lower Welford Lock

This, another 1820s improvement, is situated in the lea of Cress Hill, a short distance downriver from the Welford itself. Access by water is difficult, but a footpath leads from the village along the river bank, and offers a better route. What can be seen, when the river is not too high, are two parallel stone walls about 12 ft apart and 60 ft long. At the ends, remains of quoins which used to support the gates can be traced amidst the reeds. The speed of flow of the water in the narrow navigation channel on the opposite (north) side of the river bears witness to the continuing constricting effect of the old weir.

Grange Lock

Pilgrim lock, the next downstream from Welford, is brand new, but a little further downstream the site of Grange lock can be found. Because the navigable channel runs on the opposite side of the island to that of ancient times, little can be seen from the water. Land access is only possible by prior arrangement with the owners of Bidford Grange, but there is little to see anyway - just the typical stone-bounded, reed-choked hole.

Bidford

Barton lock (now called E.H. Billington lock) is again new, and partially makes up for the loss of Bidford water-gate. The site of the latter is reached just downstream of Bidford Bridge: weedy islands mark the line of the old weir, demolished in the 1950s in a flood prevention scheme. The old cottages at the site of Bidford Boats used to provide accommodation for boat crews (Avon barges were not lived on).

Cleeve Mill

A little downstream of the Avon's confluence with the river Arrow, under the wooded hill leading to the village of Cleeve Prior, are the remains of Cleeve Mill, its weir and associated lock. The mill, which survived until the 1930s by eeking out a living selling cream teas to water-borne tourists from Bidford (*Chapter Eleven*), has long gone. On the site of its foundations, picnickers now munch sandwiches made of flour not from such small river mills, but from immense electric food processing factories which have taken their place. Apart from the concrete slab to the north of the channel, little remains of the weir, but the site does have one of the best preserved diamond-shaped locks on the Avon. Water access is possible only by dinghy, but a walk along the main Stratford road from Robert Aickman lock affords access for explorers from large boats. The entrance to the lock can be seen from the river, high and dry since the reduction of water levels. Only from land can the ruins be really appreciated, however. Crumbling stone walls form a diamond shape characteristic of old circular locks which had been strengthened by masonry, and at the lower end of the lock is the concrete weir built to hold back the water when the old gates collapsed.

Upper Harvington Lock

This site really comprises three locks, and a derelict mill which is currently being restored. The oldest of the locks, a 70 ft circular structure, has vanished without trace under the UANT's 1969 construction. This can be found in a channel which headed sharp left beyond the weir, just before the mill building. The UANT lock was about 70 ft by 16 ft. Because of continual difficulties with silting of the lock channel, the UANT decided to construct a brand new lock to the right of the mill, and this, the Robert Aickman New lock, is the one in current use. Its predecessor has been converted into a dry-dock.

Fish and Anchor Crossing

The 'weir', which is bypassed by George Billington lock, is in fact a ford, constructed illegally by Evesham Rural District Council in the early 1900s (*Chapter Ten*). It is passable by tractors and Landrovers, walkers (with waders!) and adventurous cyclists, but *not* by ordinary cars. Crossing from the lock by means of the ford, or mooring at the 'Fish and Anchor' pub's wharf, allows access to a path leading downstream to Lower Harvington lock.

Lower Harvington Lock

This can be reached by small craft, or a footpath from the 'Fish and Anchor' (*see above*). Opposite a warning sign on the opposite side of the river, an inlet opens in the south bank. Here, water can gently flow between decaying stone walls of a rectangular chamber, now barely deep enough to float a swan but once deep enough for *Wasp* and *Bee* (*Chapter Ten*). At the lower end, gate supports survive, but at the upper end they are almost completely hidden by thick vegetation. The lock dates from the 1820s.

Redditch and Evesham Railway

This line, built by the Redditch and Evesham Company, but passing quickly into the hands of the Midland, and later the London, Midland and Scottish Railway Company, runs alongside the Avon on a steep embankment, from Cox's Bottom (the sharp left corner near Norton) to Evesham. Though it is now closed, its trains used to travel from Ashchurch (near Tewkesbury), through Evesham where they could connect with the Oxford, Worcester and Wolverhampton line, to Broom Junction. From here they could travel either north to Redditch (and Birmingham), or east along the Stratford and Midland Junction Railway. Much of the line in this area is now public footpath, though the recently built Evesham By-pass has detracted much from its charm!

Evesham

A little way beyond the railway bridge, which carries the old Oxford, Worcester and Wolverhampton Railway - the first serious competition to the Upper Avon- is Evesham Gas Works. Little now remains of the site, the last storage tanks being demolished in the mid 1980s, though some brick buildings can be seen behind the old boatyard next to the lock cut. From this gasworks, tar was loaded into barges and taken downriver to Avonmouth for resale and processing for the road industry. The freight stopped in the 1920s, due to the dilapidated state of the lower river. Just downstream of the gas works are Evesham weir and mill. The remains of punt rollers can be seen on the weir. Evesham Mill, which is now a meat processing factory, draws its power not from local water but from the national grid. There was a mill at this site since ancient times; it was a substantial concern even in the days of the Domesday Book.

Evesham lock, though of quite ordinary design, is blessed with a highly unusual keeper's house and shop, built on an 'A' frame over the sluice channel. The building dates from 1976. Almost opposite the tail of the lock channel, on the left side of the river, is the site of an old quay. This was one of several freight transhipment points on the

Bengeworth side of the river, and served Bengeworth's nail-manufacturing industry. The Workman road bridge, just beyond the aforementioned quay, is a 19th century rebuild of an earlier bridge, whose ancestor was the one demolished in the Civil War (see *Chapter Three*). To the left of the river, once it has passed under the road, are the Workman Gardens, again the remains of barge quays. A memorial to the late Douglas Barwell has recently been erected on the waterfront. Opposite the gardens is a modern block of flats built in the style of a warehouse, that stands on the site of pleasure boat yards and boatbuilders. Another old site of a pleasure boat yard is seen on the left bank just before the modern Abbey Bridge, though little remains to suggest the great activity of the place during summer months between the wars. Evesham is now changing rapidly, and landmarks are fast disappearing. The recent building of vast housing estates is overrunning the atmosphere of the rural market town, and the visitor will have to listen very carefully to hear any snatches of the famous Vale accent above the more strident tones of the industrial Midlands. New transport networks, based on fast roads to the north, have enabled 'The Dudleys', traditionally visitors in the summer months (*see Chapter Eleven*), to settle and make the place their own.

Hampton Bridges

Near a modern sewage station, the Avon is crossed by a steel railway bridge, near the stone abutments of its demolished neighbour. The demolished bridge carried the Redditch and Evesham (later Midland, later LMS) line from Evesham station across the river. The extant line takes the Oxford, Worcester and Wolverhampton (later West Midland Railway, even later, GWR) line to Worcester. The low hill on the left bank used to be covered in vineyards tended by the monks of Evesham Abbey.

Chadbury

Here is to be found one of the loveliest locks on the Lower Avon. On the right bank of the river is an old mill, again dating from before the Norman Conquest, but again converted to residential use. On the left bank is the lock, restored with the help of Royal Engineers. Unlike the locks on the Upper Avon, many of the ones on the lower are close to being in their 'original' 19th century state. The walls are of brick and stone, rather than steel piling, and the gates are wooden. Chadbury boasts the only set of traditional Avon paddle gear.

The battlemented Leicester Tower, visible looking upstream from the lock, is a folly commemorating the fall of Simon de Montfort, Earl of Leicester, in the battle of Evesham (1265).

Wood Norton

On the right bank, amongst the trees, can be seen a large BBC training college, centred around an impressive stately house with a striking golden gateway. Once the home of the Duc d'Orleans, pretender to the French throne, it was also used by the deposed King Manuel of Portugal, and became the BBC's main studios in the World War II.

Craycombe House

This, situated above a wooded corner of the river, was built by George Perrott (the younger), partly from the profits he had made on river tolls. It is still in private ownership.

Fladbury
   The home of William Sandys, this village is surprisingly hard to reach by water, there being no public mooring on the right side of the river. Fladbury boasts two mills at its weir, on opposite sides of the river. Both are now converted to houses, but that on the right bank is unusual in that it still draws power from the weir. In place of the old mill wheel is a water turbine, driving a mains generator. When it was built, the generator fed electricity to the rest of the village, giving Fladbury some of the first electrically lit streets in the county. Now the power serves only the converted mill, which is open to the public once a year when the whole village holds an open day.

Cropthorne Water-gate
   A short distance downstream of Jubilee Bridge, marked by prominent 'keep right' signs, is the site of Cropthorne water-gate where Sandys' Post once stood. On the right, there is some masonry jutting from the bank, and reed beds on the left mark the old weir (do not attempt to cross this by water).

Wyre Piddle
   The village of Wyre Piddle is seen from the water mostly as a long row of house-backs high on the right bank. The lock is, in its shape, a true survivor from the first stone locks of the river, being an almost-perfect diamond. The unusual design, while it protected the more circular earth-sided locks of Sandys time from erosion, suffers from silting because of the low flow of water in its centre. This silting blocked the river in the 1920s.
   Wyre Mill, the other side of the sluices, is now the club house of the Lower Avon Navigation Trust and their sailing club.

Pershore
   In many towns, especially those which grew up round industry, the approach by water shows their shabbiest and grimyest sides. The market town of Pershore is a pleasant exception; it turns its best side to the river. The lock is unusual in being situated on an island in the middle of the river, connected to the banks only by the weirs. It used to be circular at the top, but more rectangular deeper down, creating a trap for the unwary descending boater who had allowed his craft to stray from the centre line! On the right bank is Pershore Mill, one of the last to operate on the Avon, and the destination of *Pisgah* (Avon's last freighter). As with most of the other mills on the river, it no longer grinds corn. Below the lock cut, is the ancient bridge of Pershore on the old Aberystwyth Postal Road. In its long-suffering stones (*see Chapter Three*) are the deep grooves worn by the ropes of boatmen as they hauled their heavy barges against the stream. They merit close inspection. Just beyond the bridge are the remains of Pensham lock, the other water-gate on the Lower Avon. As at Cropthorne, no more than crumbling masonry in the banks remains.

Nafford Lock
   Almost nothing now remains of the village after which this lock was named. Bredon hill, whose gentle contours dominate the scenery to the south, suffered a great landslip in the 17th century and the original Nafford was buried almost without trace. Next to the lock, which is of typical Lower Avon design, are the great sluices of the Severn Trent water authority, used to regulate land drainage. The island is now a bird sanctuary.

Eckington Bridge
This ancient and irregularly-arched structure has stood on the site since the 16th century. Its soft stones still recall when boats were hauled with ropes, their surfaces scarred with deep grooves worn by the efforts of generations of Avon boatmen. The second bridge carries the 'Midland' line from Gloucester to Birmingham.

Strensham Lock
This lock is at the site of one of the Avon's dramatic battles, when the dispute between Sandys and Russell caused a fight over Sandys' men's boat (*see Chapter Two*). The old mill has recovered its composure in the intervening centuries, and the area is as peaceful as the rest of the river. This lock presented the LANT with its first serious problem when it became impassable in 1950/1. Its repair marked the true beginning of the restoration period, with not only the lock but also the mill house being restored to full use. Strensham lock is one of the only two mechanised ones on the river, the mechanism being installed in 1975. Its presence is a little controversial, being welcomed by many tired hire boat crews, but deplored by the river's traditionalists.

Twyning Fleet
The site of an ancient ferry over the river ('Fleet' is a derivative of 'float'), Twyning Fleet was a popular destination for hirers of Bathurst's skiffs, who would spend time at the inn before returning to Tewkesbury. The ferry, despite centuries of tradition, has fallen into disuse and the only river crossing in the area is that of the ugly M5 motorway bridge, which does much to detract from the tranquility of the area.

Tewkesbury Mills
Just after passing the boatyard, the river bifurcates, one route ('Old Avon') leading through sluices to the level of the Severn, and the other ('Mill Avon') leads to the great mills of Tewkesbury. From the early days of the abbey, corn has been ground by the power of the river here, and the town is the proud possessor of the last working mills on the Avon. These still receive much grain from the barges *Tyreley* and *Chaceley* coming from Sharpness, and the traffic constitutes all of the remaining freight carriage. Tewkesbury lock, the last on the river, has been extensively rebuilt by the LANT.

The purpose-built marina at Tewkesbury.   *Author*

Appendix Two

Addresses for Principal Waterways Restoration Groups

Lower Avon Navigation Trust
Mill Wharf
Mill Lane
Wyre Piddle
Pershore
Worcs

Upper Avon Navigation Trust
Bridge 63
Harvington
Evesham
Worcs

Inland Waterways Association
114 Regents Park Road
London
NW1 8UQ

The navigation's end - a cruiser leaves Avon Lock, Tewkesbury, bound for the Severn.
Author

Bibliography

A History of Warwick and its People, Kemp
A History of the County of Warwick Vol. 3, L. Salzman, 1945
River Navigation in England 1600-1750, T. Willan, Oxford University Press, 1936
The Turnpike Road System in England 1663-1840, W. Albert, Cambridge University Press, 1972
Thames Companion, Pritchard & Carpenter, Oxford Illustrated Press, 1975
History of the Town of Evesham, G. May, 1845
River Navigation and Trade of the Severn Valley 1600-1750, T. Willan, Economic History Review VIII, 1938
Habington's Survey of Worcestershire Vol. II, reprinted by Worcester Historical Society, 1895
The Navigation of the Avon, P. Feek, in transactions of the Birmingham Archeological Society, 1910
'Some notes on the Early Navigation of the River Avon' in *Memoirs of Old Worcestershire*, P. Feek, 1911
Collections for the History of Worcester, Nash
Wyre Piddle - the Passing Years, C. Hammond, 1972
Waterways to Stratford, Hadfield and Norris, David and Charles, 1962
England's Improvement By Sea And Land, A. Yarranton, 1676
Andrew Yarranton - the Founder of English Political Economy, P.E. Dove, Johnstone & Hunter, 1854
A Tour Through the whole island of Great Britain, Vol. II, D. Defoe, (Reprinted by Everyman's Library)
Pershore - A Short History, J. Rogers, 1977
History of Chipping Campden and Robert Dover's Olympick Games, C. Whitfield, Shakespeare Head Press, 1958
British Canals, C. Hadfield, David & Charles, 1950
Steam at Sea, K.T. Rowland, David and Charles, 1970
History of Inland Navigation, 2nd Ed., Anon., 1789
The Coal Industry of the Eighteenth Century, T.S. Ashton & J. Sykes, Manchester University Press, 1964
The New Navvies, R. Squires, Phillimore 1983
Canals of the West Midlands, C. Hadfield, David and Charles, 1966
A Guide to Stratford upon Avon, R.B. Wheler, 1814
Inland Waterways of England, L.T.C. Rolt, George Allen & Unwin, 1950
West's Directory of Warwickshire
Bentleys Directory, 1840
Rambles by Rivers - The Avon, J. Thorne, 1845
Picturesque Views on the Avon, S. Ireland, 1795
Stratford Canal Minute Book
Stratford Canal Proprietors Minute Book
Worcs & Birmingham Canal Committee Minute Book
Stratford Canal Records
Report of the Royal Commission on the canals and inland navigations of the United Kingdom, 1907-9, A8263
Slater's Directory of Worcestershire
The River Avon - Why Its Navigation Should Be Improved and How It May Be Done,

River Avon Improvement Association, 1905
Portraits of Rivers, E. Molon, Denis Dobson, 1958
Report of the Avon Committee
Heart of England by Water, W. Bliss, 1933
The Warwickshire Avon, A.T. Quiller Couch, 1892
Shakespeare's Avon From Source To Severn, C. Showell, Simpkin, Marshall, Hamilton, Kent & Co., 1901
The Idyllic Avon, J.H. Garrett, G. Putman & Sons, 1906
Working Life on Severn & Canal, H. Conway-Jones, Alan Sutton, 1990
Waterways Postcards 1900-1930, H. McKnight, Shepperton Swan, 1986
Narrow Boat, L.T.C. Rolt, Eyre & Spottiswoode, 1946
Landscape with Machines, L.T.C. Rolt, Alan Sutton, 1984
Cruising on Shakespeare's Avon, LANT, 1952
LANT AGM Minutes
The Upper Avon Navigation, D. Hutchings & D. Higgins, UANT, 1977
Race Against Time, D. Bolton, Methuen, 1990
Save the Stratford Canal!, G. Johnson, David & Charles
Stratford Council Minutes
Upper Avon Navigation 1992 report submitted to the National Rivers Authority
History of Tewkesbury , Bennet, 1830
Journey Without End, D. Bolton, Mandarin, 1987
Upper Avon Navigation Trust Report 1992
Yesterday's Town: Evesham, B. Cox & D. Alcock, Barracuda Books, 1979

Aris' Birmingham Gazette
Avon News
Beds & Bucks Observer
Berrow's Worcester Journal
Daily Telegraph
Edinburgh Philosophical Journal
Evesham Journal
Gentleman's Magazine
The Guardian
Stratford Herald
Waterways World